House Beautiful

DECORATING with
YOUR FAVORITE
OBJECTS

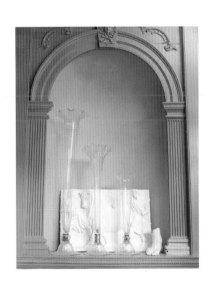

House Beautiful

DECORATING with YOUR FAVORITE OBJECTS

Elaine Louie

Photographs by Claude Lapeyre

HEARST BOOKS

A Division of Sterling Publishing Co., Inc.

NEW YORK

To my mother, Dorothy Louie,
who understands the allure of collecting.

Copyright © 2003 by
Hearst Communications, Inc.

This book was previously published as a hard-cover under the title *Collections on Display*

All rights reserved.

Produced by The BookMaker, London
Photographs by Claude Lapeyre, except for the following: page 6, Red Cover/Alain Gelberger/Inside; page 8, Red Cover/Ricardo Labougle/Inside; pages 38-39, Alexandre Bailhache; page 84, Red Cover/Ricardo Labougle/Inside; page 85, Red Cover/Ricardo Labougle/Inside; page 90, Fritz von der Schulenburg; page 91, Red Cover/Ed Reeve; page 100, Red Cover/Ken Hayden; page 101, Red Cover/Reto Guntli; and page 171, Red Cover/Ricardo Labougle/Inside.
Design by Mary Staples

Library of Congress Cataloging-in-Publication Data
Available upon request.

10 9 8 7 6 5 4 3 2 1

First Paperback Edition 2006
Published by Hearst Books
A Division of Sterling Publishing Co., Inc.
387 Park Avenue South, New York, NY 10016

House Beautiful and Hearst Books are trademarks of Hearst Communications, Inc.

www.housebeautiful.com

For information about custom editions, special sales, premium and corporate purchases, please contact Sterling Special Sales Department at 800-805-5489 or specialsales@sterlingpub.com.

Distributed in Canada by Sterling Publishing
^{c}/o Canadian Manda Group, 165 Dufferin Street
Toronto, Ontario, Canada M6K 3H6

Distributed in Australia by Capricorn Link (Australia) Pty. Ltd.
P.O. Box 704, Windsor, NSW 2756 Australia

Manufactured in China

Sterling ISBN 13: 978-1-58816-605-0
ISBN 10: 1-58816-605-8

CONTENTS

Foreword

People all across the world have a passion for collecting, but too often treasured collections are stored away in boxes or just haphazardly put in a room. Part of the fun of collecting is the joy of displaying what you've amassed. Let's face it—we could all use a little advice on how to arrange our collections. Without it, guests will simply see the clutter and disorganization that result from being out of sync with your decorating style; they won't notice or appreciate the content of your collection.

The truth is, you can tell a lot about people by the things they collect. If you walk into a house and see vintage photography prints on the walls, it's a safe bet that the homeowners have a sense of history along with an abiding interest in the camera. A collection of books clearly indicates the owners are not addicted to television, but rather, spend much of their time reading. Abstract paintings hung over antique furniture may tell you that the collectors are open-minded and don't live their lives by a formula that says everything in a room has to be one style.

In this book, author Elaine Louie does a magnificent job of telling us how to live with our collections. She not only offers advice on how to bring order to a collection, but it is clear that she has an instinctive ability to understand the diversity of collectors. So many of us tend to be somewhat shy and reserved about what we collect. On one hand, we want people to share our obsession and interests, and on the other hand, we don't quite know what to do with all the pottery, furniture, and pictures we've accumulated.

From specific ideas on how to decorate a mantel with collected objects, to advice on starting a collection, each chapter in this book is equally compelling. After all, collecting is a uniquely personal adventure. We have always advised readers to collect things that speak to them, not to simply go out and buy something because someone said it's going to be valuable, or would make a great investment. Collecting isn't about investing, it's about the great adventure of the hunt, of finding objects that have meaning to us as individuals. It's about that one chair in a far-flung corner of an antique store, or those six blue-and-white transferware plates sitting on the end of a table at a flea market. It is about living with the things we love.

—The Editors of *House Beautiful*

Introduction

When I introduced Dorothy Twining Globus, the former director of the Museum at the Fashion Institute of Technology in Manhattan, to a friend, I said, "This is an inveterate, impassioned, dazzling collector of everything: clothes hangers, globes, souvenir buildings, stamps, staplers, yellow pencils, scissors. She collects everything but lint."

Dorothy said, drily, "I considered lint." She clapped her hands. "You can turn it into felt," she said. People like her are not alone. She is a collector of the unloved things, of the eccentric, which is one kind of collector. Other people collect known objects of value such as Andy Warhol silk screens. However, what all these people have in common is the desire to amass collections of all sorts. One object, whether it is a

vintage Mickey Mouse toy or a weathervane, will not do. To a collector, the phrase "less is more" is anathema.

Collecting gives one a reason to wake up each morning, to comb the antiques magazines, browse a flea market, or an antique fair. It gives purpose to getting into bed at 9:00 P.M. in order to get up at 2:00 A.M., and slog through a muddy field to be there when the dealers pull up in their cars and vans, unfold their tables, and unwrap their wares. The early bird gets the bargain.

The collector is a curious, passionate person. The more passionate the person is, the greater is the collection. To learn about collecting you can take courses in museum studies, Chinese fine art, or surrealism. But, mostly, collectors educate themselves. They read, travel, snoop in antique

ABOVE *Primavera ceramics look fabulous on a mantel, acting as a clear focal point with their pleasing, flexible symmetry. The pieces are related, but are not twin sets. The mirror reflects a clean vista. Clutter is absent.*

ABOVE *A gilded mirror reflects the natural light pouring in from the windows. On the mantel is a grouping of personal odds and ends. The candlesticks are the only matched pair, while the other objects are related by their egg shapes, but are happily not identical.*

shops, gossip with other collectors, haunt flea markets and antique shows, and become addicted to eBay. It starts with something you covet, whether it's a nineteenth century American quilt for its history, or a Smith-Corona typewriter for its new obsolescence.

Collections, from martini shakers to pieces of tin cut like arms, legs, heads, and torsos (for supplication to saints), are tactile. As you learn about displaying objects, you begin to understand the importance of focal point, texture, variety, light, and dark.

Once you have a collection, you may or may not want to display it. Perhaps, like some collectors, you may want to hide your collection of six 1920s French watches. You may want to keep it in a jewelry box in your closet and peer into it only when you want to wear one or to show it to another watch aficionado. If you are like that, then this book is not for you.

What collections do to your home is personalize it. Along with Dorothy, the people I would like to thank for allowing us to photograph their private world are Frank Maresca, a Manhattan art dealer whose knowledge of American folk art and outsider art is astonishing; John Wilkerson, president of the board of trustees of the American Folk Art Museum, and his wife, Barbara, who have one of the most important collections of American weathervanes in the United States. Thanks also to Steven Guarnaccia and his wife, Susan Hochbaum, and many thanks to these impassioned collectors: Barry and Irene Fisher, and their architect, David Ling; Dr. Robert Lerch, Hélène Verin, Calvin Tsao and Zack McKown; Jack Masey, Clodagh and Daniel Aubry, Barbara Schubeck, Ana Daniel, Donna Schneier, Virginia Hatley, Zarela Martinez, Robert Homma, Michael Malce and Jolie Kelter, Marilyn White, Vicente Wolf, Peri Wolfman, and Charles Gold. In England, thanks to Steve and Louisa Maybury, Jacqueline Pruskin, Peter Cohen, Christine Schell, Peter Hone, Christopher Hodsell, Tom Watkins and Darren Coppin, and Jo de Banzie. In Paris, thanks to Christian Duc, Isabelle Forestier and Mattia Bonetti, Dominique Vellay, Francoise Deleu, Farfelu, and Pierre Pothier. In New Zealand, thanks to Simon and Robin Carnachan, Ron Sang, Carole Andrews, and Chrystelle Baran.

—Elaine Louie

Background
Stories
Walls

These are empty landscapes that do not have to be impersonal, or mute. Transform them into visual narratives that intrigue.

A twenty-foot-high wall was designed as a grid for a collection of African masks with shelves ten-inches deep. The background is brown, yet allows the masks to stand out. White would have been too stark a contrast. At night, three recessed lights are aimed at some of the masks.

Decorated walls of any size can tell stories of other cultures, and of moments in our own culture, and can reveal an idiosyncratic interest in detritus including childhood game boards and domestic instruments such as early rolling pins and bread boards. In reality, you can hang almost anything on a wall, which makes it the perfect background to the personal story you want to tell.

When organized, a collection becomes a focal point and makes a room come alive. The collection is also the story of the objects themselves and reveals the depth of the collector's passion. A collection can be autobiographical even when it doesn't include family photos or heirlooms, because each piece holds in it memories of a place and time.

For a collector, there is nothing more exciting than a blank, white wall. The empty area begs for display, drama, and focus. The choice then is whether to

display one huge thing—for instance, a painting, a quilt, a weathervane—or many small things, such as photographs, masks, or stitched samplers. Whatever you choose, go for drama and simplicity. You will want to catch the eye, and the simplest, least fussy display will have the boldest effect.

Think of your display as a stop sign, a visual exclamation point. Are there rules? Yes and no. Basically, it is common sense that a huge object requires its own space and that small objects require company—other like objects—so that together in a group, they become highly visible, rather than lost in space. How you place the object within a wall area is the challenge and may require some trial and error. Color, shape, scale, and texture all come into play. In this chapter, we explore how some collectors responded to the challenge of displaying their interesting, personal, and varied collections on the walls of their homes.

ABOVE *Here, two walls are a*
storyboard. On one wall, an
enormous Roy Lichtenstein
rug, bought at a Warner Bros.
store, depicts Clark Kent
ripping off his shirt. Inches
away, on the next wall, is a
Lichtenstein canvas of a
pensive and vulnerable
woman. A curvy Ron Arad
table contrasts with the
powerful lines of the pop
images. In this dining area,
dining is also an art gallery
experience.

A space may call for a particular object in the same way that a fireplace calls for chairs and sofas to face it, close-up, or a foyer calls for a mirror, for people to primp before they enter the main room. Sometimes the right choice may be to leave a wall blank as a serene empty space, a respite for the eyes, especially if the room has other, busy walls filled with memorabilia.

ORDERING A COLLECTION

Grids naturally order a collection and provide clarity, drama, and the thrill of seeing an entire collection at once. There are, however, different

OPPOSITE *Domestic Art:*
A single story on a wall.
The nineteenth century
cabbage cutter and washer
stick, for prodding laundry in
a tub, came in many homey,
whimsical variations of a
practical theme.

BELOW *An 1880s Navajo serape is called the Germantown Eye Dazzler because the dyed yarn came from Germantown, Pennsylvania. The serape warms the expanse of white while the Hopi cow mask completes the tableau.*

kinds of grids. There is the three-dimensional, built-in grid, usually a floor-to-ceiling box of shelves divided vertically into cubicles, and a visual grid, in which you simply place the objects on the wall in an orderly, gridlike fashion.

A built-in grid is a great design tool when a collection is in place. Once the measurements for a collection have been taken, there is no turning back. You have committed to that grid, a piece of custom-built furniture. However, if you have ordered shelves that are fourteen inches deep, and later, you buy something that is sixteen inches deep, you will have a problem.

Create a grid where shelves are a uniform depth. The height and width, however, can vary. You can have cubicles that are fairly uniform, or

you can have cubicles in different sizes that have room for things that are tall and thin, short and squat, or low and rectangular.

When you work with a grid, it's like playing chess. You have to anticipate what goes next to what. Does one sculpture overshadow the one next to it? Is one object so bright that the one next to it pales in comparison? Plot the arrangement on a piece of graph paper. Take into consideration the color, texture, and expressiveness of individual pieces and figure out how they work with each other in the scheme. Consider masks. Tilt a mask down, and it might look glum. Tilt it up, and it can look arrogant. Place a mask so it looks at you, eye level, and it may look cheerier than it did when it faced downward.

BELOW *A grid for this mostly Asian collection has an airy, rhythmic order. There are three adjacent shelves at the same height repeated three times.*

Every collection needs **the respite**
and relaxation of **empty space** within it.

LEFT *Two collections of Bakelite, one of large radios, the other of small figurative pieces, are displayed on adjacent walls. The radios are geometric, and arranged like architecture, facades on a streetscape. Red radios are interspersed among the yellow ones for visual rhythm and interest. The small lively Bakelite figures, at right, complement the radio collection.*

display whatever you are collecting on the wall, but in an orderly gridlike fashion.

Consider displaying paintings, photos, or art and movie posters in vertical rows, from ceiling to floor, top to bottom. The less important things can be placed at the top, and at the very bottom. It is in the larger, middle area that the eye rests in any grouping.

As a general rule, display like with like. Home art—ranging from antique wooden cabbage cutters, plastic wine racks, teapots, anything by Alessi for the kitchen, to ancient rolling pins and bread boards—makes an appealing collection, because the function of each is easily understood. Although these objects are simple, they can be idiosyncratic and witty. Collected in mass, say twenty or thirty items, they reveal a history of the domestic arts.

The kitchen is usually the obvious place to put them on a wall. By doing so, you enhance its story. The rolling pin is in its natural context. Like the objects, the display should be as simple and as unpretentious as possible.

Some objects, such as the Bakelite radios seen opposite, Matchbox toy cars, and Mickey Mouse memorabilia, are too small to require the rigid order of a grid. But they do need shelves, since they cannot be displayed dangling by a hook on a wall. The trick then is how to display similar objects and prevent the collection from being seen as one stretch of repetitive wallpaper.

Try placing the most important pieces in the middle—for instance, the biggest Mickey Mouse, the rarest Bakelite radio, or the best Matchbox car. Then play with tableau. You might want to group a Mickey with a Minnie, and pair them according to their era. Try using the brightest colors as accents. The same rule goes for any collection. Bright colors catch the eye, and focus the attention.

For flexibility, consider using adjustable shelves, adjustable stands, or mounts for your collections. For the display of African masks seen earlier in this chapter, the owner commissioned a gallery owner and expert at displaying art and art objects, to design stands with telescopic, adjustable shafts.

Remember, too, that not every cubicle has to be filled. Every collection needs the respite and relaxation of empty space within it. Objects should have air around them, so they are clearly visible front, back, and sides, and are able to be picked up and handled by guests. As people need space, so do objects.

If you do not yet have an extensive collection, do not build a three-dimensional grid. Simply

ABOVE *In a reading nook, off the open-plan kitchen, the unifying theme is food, except for the images of the faces. The side table is by Ron Arad.*

For the cars, you may want to arrange them chronologically, and play with the various colors, their silhouettes and their textures. The general feeling is: mix profiles and colors; mix sizes.

Mirrors or empty picture frames, their interior paintings lost to the ravages of time, are without doubt, collectibles. What makes the bounty of mirrors so enticing is that they are decorative. Logical rooms in which to use them include a bathroom, a powder room, or an entrance foyer, the place where you and your guests primp. (It is interesting to hang a mirror on a wall in a dining room—guests sitting opposite become obsessed with their appearance.)

However, a collection of plain, stainless steel edged mirrors would be cold and laboratory-like. They would not be sensual. The same holds true for a collection of picture frames. Without charm, something to draw out an emotional response, things remain just things.

Some collectors display frames without any pictures in them, simply for their intrinsic beauty. Ornamental frames—gilded, rococo, and hand-carved, perhaps made from natural twigs—can make an intriguing display, whereas a collection of plain, empty frames would look uninspiring. Sometimes minimalism has no effect.

When you have only three picture frames, two large and one small, put the small one in the center, either vertically or horizontally. If you're not working on an implied grid, then work with a symmetrical order in mind.

Tiles are also collectibles, whether they are handmade designs from Morocco, Iran, Italy, or the Philippines, early Dutch Delft blue and white, or made by local American craftspeople. They form a natural grid, since they are usually square, or if they are not, they can be combined into an orderly square or rectangular pattern. If they have not cracked and are waterproof, tiles work

ABOVE *Five ornamental mirrors of Venetian and Indian origins are placed in a bathroom, two placed low for children, and three high for adults. The opalescent backsplash is made of seashells transformed into tiles.*

efficiently as a backsplash in a bathroom or kitchen, or simply as an ornament on a narrow wall, a foyer, a door panel. They can also run along the top of a molding to add more visual effect.

You can also use two adjacent walls to tell the story of a single material. For instance, one wall can be devoted to Bakelite radios, the adjacent

ABOVE *In this cool bathroom is a collection of distorted images, all shot by Weegee, the photographer best known for crime-scene reporting. Looking at the photos, and then at yourself, could lead to some disturbing existential reckonings. The open teeth on top of the sink are another hint that life can be raw and raucous. In this bathroom's display of photos and teeth, beauty is particularly illusory, and irony is key.*

one to tiny Bakelite figures. Or, one wall can feature large hooked rugs, and a second wall, smaller rugs. One wall can show 1940s posters, while the adjacent wall can happily display a collection of well-preserved 1940s cigar box labels. The story will be variations on a theme. They will complement, not compete with, each other.

FIXED OR FLEXIBLE?

Some displays, once they have been assembled, are fixed and locked in place precisely because they tell a story with a beginning, middle, and end, or at least with a major piece of drama. When a collector devoted an entire wall to nineteenth century American weathervanes, most by Jonathan Howard, she started with a focal point, an Indian with bow and arrow. It is tall, lively, and full of grace. She placed it dead center, and then built around it, leaving lots of white space between a pig, horse and rider, and fish. Each item's silhouette is clear. She also created action. Horses seem to be riding toward each other. A figure with the flag reaches toward the Indian. Thus dialogues are created between most figures.

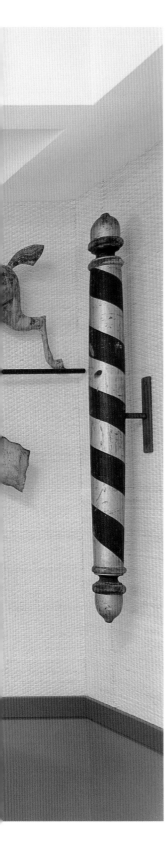

The pig and fish, however, ignore the entire business, and head off in a separate direction. If she were to change just one figure, the entire narrative would lose steam.

You, too, can achieve a wall like this if you take the time to look closely at each piece you own and work out the narrative before starting to arrange it. You will be inspired by the secret story hidden behind each antiquity and come to the right storyline both for the collection and for the wall space. It might take you a day or more to sort it out; however, the effort will pay off in an intriguing wall display.

For example, let's say you are about to work with photographs of athletes—skiers, deep-sea divers, and perhaps equestrians. Once you juxtapose them to look their liveliest (they are athletes, after all, not still lifes of fruit) you may have locked yourself into a permanent display. Remove one element, and the entire display may crumble, and you will have to reassemble the display from scratch.

On the other hand, reworking a collection is part of the delight. A home is not an institution that pledges itself to display the Mona Lisa, the Elgin Marbles, or Washington Crossing the Delaware in the same place, year after year. One item in the collection may have been half hidden for the past six months and you might decide that now is the time for its fifteen minutes of fame as the focal point of the collection.

Some displays are extremely flexible, like the collection of obis on this page. The owner has hung four patterned obis, all orange and white but in

RIGHT *The owner placed a Martin Munckacsi photo of flamenco dancers on an easel, and flanked it with two Ming-style chairs. The wall acts as a backdrop. In a large room, this kind of display makes the room more intimate, and provides seating for a tête-à-tête.*

different patterns, on a wall from floor to ceiling. A few inches of empty space separates one obi from another, giving the viewer the impression that part of the wall is striped. Empty space is necessary so that the design of each obi stands out. Yet there shouldn't be so much white space that the coherence disappears. Gauging the right distance is rather like figuring out how far to stand from another person at a cocktail party. Near, but not too near.

When individual items are very small, you need to get up close to appreciate them, even when they are displayed en masse. Thus the rule of thumb is to leave lots of floor space clear in front of the collection. It is best not to obstruct the view with pieces of furniture.

Collecting is **shopping with a purpose.** Having a category in mind makes shopping a **sport.**

RIGHT *These four Bill Traylor prints are small. On a big wall, they would be lost. However, when they are framed identically, and placed in a grid, they become a focal point.*

DISPARATE COLLECTIONS ON ONE WALL

It is much harder to display several, disparate collections on one wall than a collection devoted to a single subject. It requires more thinking. The trick is to make tiny groupings within the larger display. Say you have a half-dozen Edward Weston photographs, four of your children's drawings, and a dozen antique St. Valentine cards. Consider framing the photographs in a plain silver frame, the children's drawings in simple wood frames, and the antique valentines in one large velvet frame. Then create one grid for the photos, another for the drawings, and place the valentines, which together might form the largest rectangle, in the center.

In a kitchen, you might have a display of homely utensils: 1940s ceramic mixing bowls, 1950s pitchers, and a dozen illustrations of sunbonnet babies. Frame the babies, grouping them together. Put the pitchers next to one other and the bowls too. Organize the pitchers by descending order, or big one in the middle, and then symmetrically descending order. Tilt the spouts the same way so that the silhouettes echo one another. The bowls can also be organized by descending order or with the biggest in the middle. What unifies these disparate collections are the silhouettes.

Some people choose a color that appeals to them, for example, red, and collect things in that color family—glassware, plates, and flea market portraits of ladies in red. Again, group like with

LEFT *Rough on smooth:
Four textured wool panels on
a bare white wall, together
with the striped bedspread
and the stack of books by the
headboard, create a
horizontal sweep across
the room.*

OPPOSITE *Rough on rough:
The owners of this Manhattan
loft like strong, powerful,
rugged shapes, whether they
are masks, bowls, or pots from
Asia, Africa, or South America.
They left the exterior brick
walls unpainted, and painted
the interior walls. A brick wall
in the living room is the
rough-hewn background for
several African masks.*

like. Put shades of red that work best with one another. Keep in mind that a purplish red will not necessarily look good with an orangey red.

For inspiration, go to a flower shop, and see how white lilacs are mixed with white tulips and white anemone. Look at shades of color, mixes of textures, and silhouettes—pointy with round, spiky with limp. This will give you notions on how to put objects next to one another.

TEXTURE

Walls have texture, whether they are sheetrock smooth, rough as old brick, cold as cement, translucent, or, transparent as glass. When you have a smooth texture, anything can be displayed against it, for example, a nineteenth century silk embroidery, a painting, or a Hudson Bay blanket.

ADJACENT WALLS

Using two adjacent walls as a storyboard is a possibility for works of art, as long as you can relate one to another. If you have three walls, consider a triptych, so long as there is the relief of negative space—a blank wall, an open door, or a window. When you're working with adjacent walls, be sure that the collections don't compete with each other in color, texture, and content.

THAT ONE THING

You can display just one thing on a wall when it is large enough and bold in its design. It has to be eye-catching, since it will be seen from a distance, and should have some kind of importance, either historically or sentimentally. The item could be great-grandmother's handmade crazy quilt, that

LEFT *The owner of this home, a London-based antiques dealer, has transformed the stair landing of his home into a photo gallery. The images are organized in a subtle grid. Small photos descend vertically on the right. A large horizontal photo sets the boundaries of those arranged below. The photo on the floor gives the arrangement a spontaneous feeling.*

OPPOSITE *A skinny male fertility figure with its joyous outstretched arms sits in a narrow corner of a Manhattan home. The verticality of the figure and the space seem to be a perfect fit.*

would never fetch much money at auction, but has great sentimental value for both you and the family and a pleasing pattern.

That one thing can be a reproduction of a Medieval tapestry, a delicate Chinese scroll painting, or a giant blowup of a very endearing photograph of your child's face at age two. It can be a warrior's shield placed on a narrow wall at the end of a corridor.

Whatever you select, make sure it has impact and fills the space but does not dominate it.

BACKGROUND FOR SMALL THINGS

Some collections are not large enough to take up an entire wall. Still, sometimes a wall can act as a background for a small thing. What's essential is to frame it dramatically, to make a small object or a few small objects stand out.

You can frame a picture, sketch, or sampler architecturally by placing it between windows, columns, or within a niche. You could also place it on a door at the end of a narrow corridor. Place it where it cannot be missed. Use the architecture

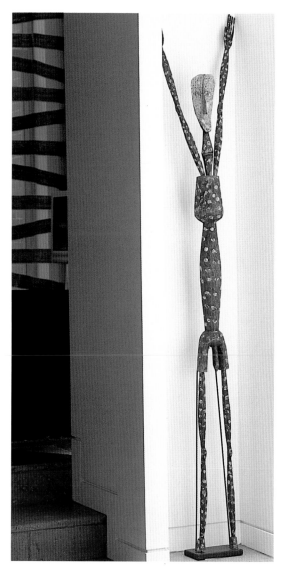

Framed photographs or **art prints** placed **casually** against a wall introduce **informality** to a grouping.

RIGHT *The owners of this Oxfordshire home have two daughters and use the stairwell as a revolving gallery for photographs of the children and also the children's photographs of their parents. Since all the photographs are in the same size frames, they are interchangeable and can be moved around.*

LEFT *In this Paris home, the owners placed Chinese Canton enamel dishes, as well as a framed Islamic textile, above an eighteenth century oak door.*

of your home. If there is a niche, fill it. If there is molding going in a rectangle, put more framed rectangular prints, photos, or samplers within.

Take the mullions of your window and repeat the shape on a wall by framing drawings, new or antique embroideries, or cartoons in frames the same dimensions as the mullions.

When there's only a single object that is not large enough to take up a wall, but is important enough to have attention lavished upon it, placing it on a stand, pedestal, or easel can make it more dramatic. Then you can frame it by placing a pair of chairs, urns, or tall potted plants on either side.

BELOW *A bathroom is given that extra touch of glamor with trompe l'oeil walls acting as a large frame to the collection of framed prints hanging above the bath.*

ABOVE *This wall feels as if it has seen a thousand centuries pass by, whereas it is covered in modern plaster molds made from the originals. As a display, it speaks of careful planning so that each piece has the space it requires to make an impact.*

OPPOSITE *In this elegant London drawing room you might be forgiven for thinking you had wandered into a seaside museum. The two walls framing the large window are covered with framed and glass-front boxes of shells. There are many more boxes in the charming seashell collection which the owner bought on a whim.*

ABOVE *Extra storage and display space was created by building shelves across the top of a window. Shoji screens conceal or reveal the collection of bottles from England, China, France, Holland, and the United States. They are organized by color: green on top, blue below. An American poison bottle has ridged sides, and on a dark night, you could feel that it still contains the poison.*

LEFT *The owner of this apartment, a Manhattan interior designer, is willing to let natural light fade a black and white photograph. Double urban landscapes, one photographic, one real, are juxtaposed with the fresh, bright greens in the vase.*

When you have a rough texture like exposed brick, putting something smooth against it may look too high contrast. The smooth object, for example, a flag, may look very clean against a dirty background. Exposed brick is seldom immaculate, even when whitewashed. There can be holes, dents, and crumbly corners that are not necessarily very attractive. Preferably, put rough things against a rough background, such as carved African masks, weathervanes, a fabulous feathered headdress from Cameroon, or original Aboriginal art against a brick wall.

Awkward spaces—a staircase landing, the ledge above a doorway, and a niche in a wall—are good places to put a collection, because no one expects something there. The collection becomes a surprise. Climbing up a flight of stairs becomes an adventure when pictures, maps, or hooked rugs line the walls of the landing.

In Europe, there's a tradition of putting things like Chinese porcelain above doors and above cupboards that dates from the seventeenth century. The reason for this awkward display site? There was not a lot of furniture (a.k.a. display

RIGHT A London antiques dealer created a faux stained glass window by hanging turquoise, blue, and yellow resin replicas of Coadestone, eighteenth century architectural ornaments made from an artificial stone. He suspends the replicas on wire, and centers them within each pane of glass.

space) then. Overdoors, which was the expression, were the places where people put precious objects even though they were not easily visible. Overdoors are also where children could not get to fragile treasures.

WINDOW AS WALL

As a natural backdrop, windows are walls of light. Like walls, windows can frame a collection of many similar items, or one single, large object. By putting a collection of glass—snifters, glasses, bottles, vases, inkstands, panels of stained glass—in front of a window, the light will bring out the transparency, colors, and patterns of the glass. The colors will shift during the course of the day,

RIGHT *The owners collect old pottery jars from Spain, Greece, China, and Italy, and display them on a windowsill in their home. They choose them for their humanlike forms and drape the jars with examples of their ethnic jewelry.*

cobalt becoming almost black. At night, you might need to amplify the light with pin lights, or back lights.

A collection in front of a window also helps to obscure an unfortunate view and affords the residents some degree of privacy. Just as natural light enhances glass, it will fade textiles and photographs, so take advice when considering placing these types of items in full daylight.

FRAMING

If a collection lends itself to being framed, as do samplers, art posters, and art photographs, you can do as many museums do, and choose identical frames and mats for visual unity. This creates a symmetry and a harmony wherever you decide to place the display.

The other solution is to put everything in completely different frames of a similar material,

LEFT *A collection of gourds and ceramic teapots shaped like gourds stands on a glass shelf against a window. The appeal of the gourds lies in their voluptuousness. They bulge, twist, and arch.*

LEFT *An eclectic niche, an altar of sorts, was created in a corner of this home. The arched window dates from the fourteenth century, and the door is nineteenth century, with a carved bas relief of the holy grail. A Santo Nino, a baby Christ from the Philippines, sits on the window sill.*

and hang them in an orderly way. One frame could be gilt, another silver, and a third bronze-tinted. Or, if you chose frames made of wood, one could be rectangular, another round, and another oval in shape. The same goes for velvet, bamboo, stitched, or pewter frames. The variety of shapes lends a richness to the display, and implies that the collection was brought together over time from different places.

LEFT *The bull weathervane, which was made in Wisconsin, used to perch on a dairy barn. The owners carried it first to the living room, the dining room, and finally to the bathroom, where it stands framed by an enormous window and surrounded by plants. The bull looks as if it is roaming in an exotic jungle.*

At the bottom of each plant, to the right, is a label which gives the scientific and common name, the species, the genus, the date it was collected, and the uses of the herbal plant. Most of the plants were collected in a forest near Seine et Oise, France, in 1917.

In the Picture

This herbier, in the bedroom in a chateau belonging to shoe designer Christian Louboutin, has been displayed in an innovative manner. He bought the 300-plant collection, the passion of a Monsieur Schoeller, at a sale and approached Loïc Dolléans to work out a way of displaying them. He did not want to relegate the collection to a dusty shelf or hide them away in a casket, because he was fascinated by the quality of the collection and the detail of the plants collected by Schoeller in his spare time from 1913 to 1920.

Christian wanted to be able to admire them at his leisure. Over several days, one hundred plants were selected and a plan was worked out to give them a graphic cohesion. He discerned there were several styles in the final collection, romantic, abstract, and figurative, and decided to regroup them for display by genre. On one wall is a family of eighteenth century poppies and thistles, on another are herb pictures with forms reminiscent of Japanese calligraphy. The plants are an integral part of the wall, attached by an adhesive that allows them to be moved later if so desired. The partition is made of timber and is distanced from the wall by plots, an ingenious idea that guarantees the flow of air needed to conserve the framed herbs. The cornice is sited out from the wall, and the framed plants are held in spaces cut to exact measurements.

OPPOSITE *The collection of hundred-year-old herbs in this brilliantly conceived wall display is on the wall of shoe designer Christian Louboutin's bedroom. Each plant is held in place by silicone, so it may be replaced in time with another if necessary.*

Treasured
Islands
Tabletops

Some tables have **strict daily uses**.
Others do not and lend themselves
to displaying **precious things**.

*Shells, stones, and flowers make a natural display on this marble-topped
side table placed just before a doorway so it provides a pleasant visual
surprise as people walk in and out of the room.*

A table is an ancient piece of furniture that has found its way into our hearts. Greeks and Romans decorated rooms with tables, tripods, and sideboards and used them just as we do now. They ate from their tables, displayed gold and silverplate on their sideboards, and put braziers on tripods, sometimes as offerings to the gods. What we now call console tables were attached to walls, and they used trestle tables to display marble objects and other smaller and portable works of art.

By the Middle Ages, game and writing tables had made an appearance in various rooms. Library tables, dressing tables, occasional tables, and coffee tables gradually found a place in the home, too. Imagine how many *billets doux* (letters of love), filled with dreams, were written on tables during Jane Austen's and Edith Wharton's time? If only a tabletop could tell the tales that were written in the privacy of one's room . . . .

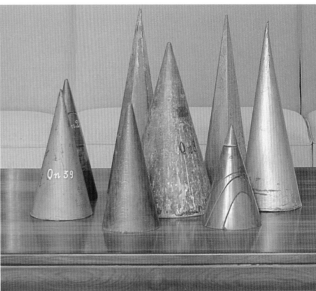

Today, people do not necessarily use a table according to its original intent.
A trestle, once made for an Irish farmhouse kitchen, now finds itself in a
Manhattan loft with a rusted iron sculpture on its rugged surface, out of its
time, but perfectly at home in its new environment.

As in antiquity, modern tables have dedicated everyday uses. Other tables
break away from this strict daily regime and lend themselves to the display
of seashells, sprays of coral, vases, urns, and tribal masks. In a decorating
scheme, think of tables as pedestals or display stands, whether they are a
lowly coffee table, a rectangular plinth, or a sideboard. These essential pieces
of furniture can be as informal as a 1930s wood and rattan plant stand, or a
lonely bar stool repainted cobalt blue, gleaming black, or lipstick red, and as
ornamental as an Indian chest inlaid with mother-of-pearl.

In this chapter you will discover just how exotic a tabletop can look.

OPPOSITE *The hawk is the fierce, irresistible focal point in this tableau on an eighteenth century oak table from Castle Howard. The display is another chapter in the story of Coadestone, an eighteenth century artificial stone used for architectural ornament in England. The hawk is from a gate pier, and the other Coadestone artifacts are grouped like with like in strict symmetry.*

LEFT *Two architectural images on the wall, and a rhythmic grouping of glass decanters on the table below. What unifies the two displays is an airy transparency and strong vertical silhouettes. The lamp is another vertical element.*

BELOW *The owner of this delight first found the nineteenth century cast iron fish tank, then the twentieth century cast iron aquarium stand with the seahorse legs, and finally, the wind-up snail toys. Voilà! An underwater story.*

What all tables require when used as a background to a display is sturdiness. Some interior designers think about a table as a wall, treating it as a flat plane on which to reveal a story in time.

Just as the use of a table has shifted over the centuries, so, too, what we place atop it has changed. A table, by its size, shape, material, and style, has its own personality. It can suggest what kind of collection looks best on it.

This process begins with the size, scale, and placement of the table. Second, its use. Is the table purely decorative, is it a side table, a place to put a book and a lamp? Third, consider scale. The bigger and heavier the table, the bolder the objects on top ought to be. For example, a wood trestle table calls for big objects, rustic or ethnic, such as tactile hand-carved wood bowls or vessels of different shapes. The table might be an English farm table, and the bowls might be African, yet the confluence

of oversized, strong shapes and the same thick, sturdy material—wood—works as a display.

On the other hand, the objects do not have to be made of the same material as the table. Large woven baskets, whether made in the American South, Japan, or France would look equally well on a rustic table. With that combination, there is a unity of highly textured materials. The baskets can hold their own and will not disappear.

Neither will collections of utensils disappear. Copper pots and pans, bamboo steamers which come stacked, and pewter pitchers look natural and unforced when placed on a large table surface in a kitchen or dining area.

In a foyer, a large round, square, or rectangular table of a beautifully finished wood like cherry or mahogany can look amazing with a huge, soaring bird cage placed in its center. An antique bird cage is airy, whether made of metal, wood, or bamboo, but if it is two-and-a-half to three feet high, it will be a strong yet delicate object and create the perfect focal point in a large entrance foyer.

A MATTER OF SCALE

Tabletops can accommodate smaller-scale objects that walls sometimes cannot. The small objects can be functional or purely decorative. They can be ashtrays, cigarette boxes, and pitchers.

Or they can be a grouping of paper fans, jade amulets, and ivory, each one a decorative yet nonessential object.

OBJECT PLACEMENT

What is alluring about a tabletop display is its proximity and tactility. Objects within our reach are there to be fondled and admired by passersby. Before placing objects, think about how they will look. Create a pattern. Perhaps on a round table, the smaller objects should be arranged in a circle around the large ones. On a rectangular table, a gridlike pattern can be appealing. Design the collection so all the little parts become part of a coherent whole with the major piece dominating.

If shells and stones are scattered nearby, place them casually, keeping in mind a natural beauty. Try not to clutter the shells and stones, but group them artfully, with a bit of air or empty space between. Try to create a subtle symmetry. Mounds

RIGHT A London dealer grouped African-inspired ceramic designs from Atelier Primavera, the design studio of Au Printemps, the French department store, on 1950s French plant stands. Their angularity complements the silhouettes of the squirrel and zebra.

BELOW Glazed blue jars and vases, sensually round, sit on lacquered red tablemats placed on a large table to create different heights for the display.

LEFT *Here, the the warmth of a wood frame contrasts with the cool silvery surface of an aluminum-faced sideboard. Curvy pottery pieces are juxtaposed with the geometric pattern of the sideboard. The mirror reflects another collection across the room.*

OPPOSITE ABOVE AND BELOW *Objects that cross cultures are displayed on an Art Deco tray. Most of the objects are from natural materials, either left raw or designed. A yellow glazed ceramic egg has been placed in a carved amber bowl from Malaysia, which looks like plastic. A carved jade bowl, when held up to the light, is translucent. There are also shells, nuts, and an African bracelet.*

of seashells may emulate nature, but they do not look good on a tabletop. Most seashells are beautiful, but some are more beautiful than others. Think of the voluptuous curves of a conch shell and the flatness of a sand dollar. Some may find the former cute, others the latter. Discard imperfect shells because they can spoil the effect. Another type of collection you often see is one based on a single material, such as mother-of-pearl, silver, or pewter. Silver boxes of different shapes and

sizes, whether they are oblong, square, rectangular, hexagonal or heart-shaped, can look good together in a group.

When dealing with really small items such as antique buttons, teaspoons, tiny sea shells, or small smooth pebbles, the rule remains: The most important one goes center, or at the top of the table, and the remainder are then arranged in order of diminishing importance with an eye to varying silhouettes, textures, and shapes.

CREATING FOCAL POINTS

Like all displays, there should be a focal point, a theme, a strand of connective tissue. Following are a few good basic rules to consider.

- Isolate what's in the center and point out the levels of importance. What's highest, biggest, and most fascinating is clearly the most important and goes in the center. What's on the perimeter is less important. This surface is not a landing place for miscellany. It is not where you toss the house keys, the bills, and the Chinese take-out menus.

- When you have lots of little things, keep them at a low angle, or on a low table.

- As you group the objects, which could be anything from carved Buddhas and scholars' rocks to Russel Wright dishware, consider heights, rhythm, variation, and silhouettes.

- Think of a physical landscape with mountains and valleys. Put the flattest, smallest pieces on the perimeter. These are the supporting pieces to the central object.

- Natural things, such as stones, seashells, and fossils, are obvious pieces to collect and are gathered by both children and adults. One way of displaying them on a table is to center the display with a shell-framed mirror, a piece of art made of shells, or a gigantic seashell, so enormous and so beautiful as to dazzle.

OPPOSITE, CLOCKWISE FROM LEFT
Gleaming glass objects are placed together. Pens are in a glass container, and leather-bound books are stacked horizontally for easy access. One hundred opal eggs in an off-white ceramic dish enhances the soft, shifting colors of the eggs. A kitsch collection of glitter fruit, styrofoam balls stuck with pins and sequins, vye for the eye inside a kitschy glittery basket.

With silver, place a filigree box next to a solid one which, in turn, can be placed next to an etched one. The final collection will have the material as its link, and the intrinsic beauty of each box will shine.

PATTERNED TABLETOPS

Mother-of-pearl is commonly used as inlay on boxes and has also been used as a decoration on table surfaces. If you own a table with a highly patterned surface, you should not put small or patterned things on it. The objects will get lost in all that visual activity.

Instead, place strong, solid-color tall things on the patterned table, such as candlesticks, books, sculpture, vases, and lamps. The objects on the patterned tables should be vertical, so that you focus your eye on them without being distracted by the patterned table. The aim is for the objects and the table to be in harmony with each other, not in competition.

CHOOSING THE TABLE

Sculptors such as Brancusi believed that the base was integral to the sculpture. Thus, if you consider your tablescape to be a small-scale sculpture, the base becomes a thing of importance. You have several choices.

If it is simply to be used as background, and may even be obscured by the collection, choose a neutral table, a plain table that is at least presentable. However, if the table is an important element and is visible as a horizontal frame for the collection, then you should think about whether to match it to your collection or to use it as a juxtaposition to your display.

If you choose to match the collection to the table, unify the two elements by era. For example, place an Art Deco vase on a sleek Art Deco table; perch a Victorian taxidermy owl on a Victorian polished wood table with a pedestal base, or a

collection of 1940s toasters on a 1940s enamelled white table with a little red trim. Ceramics from the 1920s can perch on 1920s flower pot stands.

You can also unify by material. For example, marble architectural fragments could find sublime happiness on a marble table.

Alternatively, you could contrast a collection against the table's surface. Placing a basket of bright beaded fruit on a white Parsons table puts kitsch against white modernism. Or, putting a collection of glass pitchers, tall and thin, fat

and squat, on a round oak table with a base of carved lion's feet creates a contrast between solid and fragile.

Other juxtapositions might include a collection of silver vases, forks, and spoons on a Victorian rosewood table, or conversely, Victorian valentine cards on a Mies van der Rohe table. Ivory boxes, cigarette holders, and picture frames would look sensual and inviting on a mahogany table. The warm brown wood would set off the ivory. If the table is a solid color, solid-colored objects or

ABOVE *A collection of African masks is placed at different heights in what appears to be a casual, natural cluster. The table has some empty space, enough for two people to gather around the table.*

What is a tray but a **portable table** for your portable collection of **treasures?**

LEFT *Pewter unifies this tabletop display of unrelated late nineteenth to early twentieth century objects on a marble-topped wrought iron table in the home of a London photographer. The arrangement is intimate and highly personal.*

patterned ones would be suitable. There are
choices. You can work monochromatically and put
white vases on white tables or white vases on
cream. Likewise, you could put pewter objects on
an aluminum table, and mercury balls (on a tray)
on a mirrored table; exotic timber boxes with a
lustre finish on a highly polished timber tabletop.

If you want to work with color, you could place
a fragile, but big, lettuce-shaped green tureen on a
blue table, mindful of the dictum: blue and green
should never be seen. Bright orange California
pottery would work on a red Parsons table. A
collection of vases filled with blue flowers would
be lovely on a gray table with a flaking surface.

ABOVE *On this Thonet table,
the focal point is a porcelain
Mao figure surrounded with
people. In front of Mao, the
Parisian owner has arranged
a casual but neat collection
of Mao buttons. The other
items are the doll and the
two dogs, which frame the
Mao statue. The symmetry is
implicit, not obvious.*

LEFT *In a small apartment,
leather-bound books are
grouped in horizontal piles on
the desk. They are
first editions of classics.
Because the books are
beautifully bound, they work
as a tabletop display.*

ABOVE *In this still life, small
categories of objects are
arrayed in a suggested slanting
grid on a tray. To what would
be an array of tactile objects,
an ominous crocodile and a
lush orchid were added, creating a tropical scene.*

SINGLE OBJECT, SINGLE TABLE

Some objects require their own table, like a fantastic sculpture of a person, an enormous toy robot, or a huge Korean celadon bowl. Things that are round look well isolated on a pedestal, plinth, or on a small table. People can then move around it, look at it from every angle, and see the details of the item up close.

If you have a collection of busts, mechanical robots, or beautiful bowls, you might want to buy, or have made, a set of plinths and put one object on each plinth. Whether the plinths are the same size and height depends on the collection. Sometimes a collection looks good when each object is the same size and placed on the same height plinth. The contrary solution is to display each of the items on plinths that are different heights for a more dynamic presentation. When in doubt, draw the design on a piece of graph paper, study and manipulate it until you achieve the desired effect.

PATTERNED & DISPARATE ITEMS

Patterned objects are harder to display than those in a solid color. When they are displayed together, patterned objects should have some kind of relationship—either they are made by the same artist, such as Art Deco pottery by Clarice Cliff, or they have similar colors. Or perhaps they are the same object, such as a teapot, but with a different interpretation. There should be lots of empty space around each of them, too.

BELOW LEFT *Here is part of a collection of more than 500 bottles designed between 1910 and 1950. What unifies the collection are the Bakelite caps and highly graphic labels. Cologne, perfume, and lotion bottles are located around the bathtub.*

Calvin Tsao and Zack McKown, of Tsao McKown, Manhattan architects, collect what Mr. Tsao calls "synergies—things that cross cultures, like a carved amber bowl from Malaysia, a jade bowl from China, and a bronze bowl from Sweden." They choose exceptionally sensual things, whose patina and surfaces are partly the result of having been touched for centuries. Colors are key, but the architects order the collection by placing them in a lacquered tray.

Everyday items such as glasses, beakers, pitchers, and ashtrays, become interesting when nonchalantly grouped together with alternating rhythms of shapes and heights. In the kitchen, there is nothing that can't be grouped together and stuck into big glass cylinders. Whether your

utensils are gleaming or matte stainless steel, silver plate, or sterling silver, they look sculptural and festive. The utensils will be handy when each type of tool is given its own glass cylinder.

All kinds of dishes, such as decanters, cocktail shakers, and even mixing bowls, naturally lend themselves to being together. They have such appealing shapes and textures.

There are, however, thousands of ways to arrange a collection of pitchers, for example. (See page 114.) Take a bunch of white ones, all different, but all basic pitchers. They can face each other as if they were in conversation. They can all face the same direction. They can descend horizontally from tall to short. It can be fun to arrange and rearrange these whenever the moment takes you.

BELOW CENTER *This display explores the possibilities of design within a single context: the blue pitcher. The cobalt blue ceramic pitcher is Portuguese, the one with the fluted top is American, and the tall speckled one at the rear, Scandinavian.*

BELOW RIGHT *Try placing all your knives in one glass container, the forks in another, and the spoons in yet another. Lined up on display, they'll have impact.*

ORDERING A TABLESCAPE

Some collections, such as pitchers, hand blown Venetian glass, papier-mâché, or stone eggs, and scientific instruments look best not in a complex tablescape but in a casual cluster. Other objects, especially round ones like antique Christmas tree ornaments, a child's collection of glass marbles, antique billiard balls, or antique silver chopsticks, will roll about unless contained.

Muppet buttons (yes!) might be best displayed on a tray to contain them. Glitter fruit (sequins stuck into Styrofoam balls shaped like apples, bananas, and oranges usually made by ten-year-old girls) take a basket, even a glittery, kitsch basket. Kitsch looks best gathered together because it makes a firm statement. Display it with

suitable brash abandonment. Remember one person's idea of what is kitsch is another's idea of style. In collecting, passing judgment on matters of taste is out of bounds.

Sometimes a collection consists of insignificant objects (made significant, of course, by the sheer fact you are collecting them), and there isn't any one major piece. In this case, lay them out on a flat surface and apply an editor's eye to the pieces. Are there any which look out of place with the others? Are any too big for the tabletop you have in mind?

Are there any whose color is a hue or two off balance with the rest of the pack? Be strong and discard any item you feel will not add something to the display. Look for a few pieces that, together, will make a major centerpiece. Use the size, color, and texture design guidelines discussed in other chapters. You might find there are actually two collections within the items you are hoarding. In that case, look around for another display site, hopefully in another room. Too much of the same thing in one place can be detrimental.

ABOVE *An Empire State Building made of Lincoln Logs is the focal point of this large living room. It is placed strategically, so that it not only centers the room, but it is also reflected in a mirror. A collection of watering cans is to the left of the building.*

RIGHT *This collection of staplers dates from the nineteenth century. Some of the staplers have scorpion-like tails, which held the staples. Like many industrial designs, the stapler has been miniaturized and made sleek in the course of a century of use.*

Do you have tall and slender items that require something to show them off? Look for tall cylinders to use as storage, and use your imagination when choosing them. In Shanghai, at the DR Bar, antique cricket ticklers—long thin pieces of bamboo with hairs at the end that were used for tickling crickets to provoke them to fight—are used as martini stirrers. The ticklers, hairs pointing in the air, are stored in ceramic jars designed to hold two crickets. Another option is to find two or three of the beautiful wood cylinders that Chinese scholars have traditionally used to store their calligraphy brushes.

Antique leather-covered cylinders, modern brushed or shiny stainless steel cylinders, and smooth wood designs will each provide a unique place for something you have in your home that doesn't have a place to call its own. Be careful not to overload them—remember less is more and they will not topple over.

PHOTOS ON TABLETOPS

When grouping family snapshots, or perhaps Brassai's classic scenes of Paris, there's always the question of whether or not to match the frames. The same schools of thought that apply to framing things for the wall apply equally to frames on a table. The easiest is to put all of them in the same type of frame, although in different sizes. Choose a single material—wood, gilt, velvet, silver, or pewter—and put every picture in the same frame. For example, wood, but make sure each frame looks completely different, maybe from different eras, or some might be smooth, others might be ridged or patterned. This will ensure a visual and textural interest.

Heights of framed images should vary, as they do in nature. (Have you ever seen shrubs and flowers growing to exactly the same height?) When framing an image, select a mount that will not suffocate it and lessen its impact.

OPPOSITE *Nineteenth century mathematical instruments for measuring are placed together on a 1950s Danish rosewood table. The eye tends to ignore the painting on the wall and focus attention on the far more interesting architectural model of a mosque.*

LEFT *The owner of this Manhattan house collects all things Mexican. In her living room, nearly everything is part of a collection, from the candlesticks on the table to the serapes on the sofa. She casually drapes the serapes vertically on the sofa, and by overlapping them, and placing the pillows on them she weights the serapes down so they don't rumple and slip around.*

LEFT *The owners of this eclectic collection created a bold, rhythmic, extravagant display of baskets by placing them not only on the top of the chest, but on the knobs, and on a chair. They juxtaposed the handcrafted baskets with photography. Each basket evokes a memory of a place they have visited.*

TELLING STORIES

A tablescape, if long enough, can recount an entire epic. You can recreate the evolution of birdhouses with a collection of birdhouses made in China, England, France, and Italy. You could do the same with dollhouses and intersperse them with dolls of the period, dining, laying around, and strolling. People who collect souvenir buildings tend to naturally gravitate to clustering buildings of a certain type and/or city together. In other words, you can re-create your own tiny cityscape of Paris, London, or Manhattan.

PERSONAL VS. "DESIGNED"

Some collections look intensely personal by the way they're grouped. The objects could be seashells, paint-by-number paintings, miniature chairs, and somehow in the display, they look as though the owner amassed them lovingly over the years, and in a day or two or three, fiddled with them until somehow they looked right.

These collections look lived-in. Other collections look designed. They reveal not the hand of the collector, but of the interior designer. They are not less appealing just because they are professionally designed.

The collector who has a passion for an object but not an eye for visual display does exist. So an interior designer who is asked to organize the collection is no different than the museum curator or the director of exhibitions.

A chic collection, one that's highly graphic in its arrangement and seems to exist somewhat apart from the rest of the home, still has a point. It focuses the eye, offers a lesson in history or design and warms a room.

A London-based interior designer had a client who had a collection of cones, nineteenth century mathematical instruments that come apart and are used as measuring tools, but the client had

ABOVE *The owners of this toy collection layer photographs one behind the other, but alternate heights and shapes of frames so photographs peek out enticingly from behind others. The focal point, however, is the blue and green truck.*

displayed them singly and in isolation. He also had a mahogany architectural model of a mosque, whose dome lifts off to reveal columns inside. The designer grouped all the cones together on a 1950s Danish rosewood table so the collection became a focal point (see page 60). He also juxtaposed the nineteenth century cones against the mid-century modern table, to create an unexpected effect. To make the mosque a focal point, he hung a "slightly boring painting" over the mosque to draw attention to the model, which would have looked very small against the bare wall. He tried displaying the mosque on the table against the wall without the painting, and it seemed lost.

LEFT *In this Paris living room, a focal point is a gilded wood sculpture made by Annie Ratti. Mattia Bonetti's pair of upholstered twig chairs, which he designed for a show of textiles designed by Manuel Canovas, frame the table display. Because the chairs are fragile they have been placed behind the sofa so they won't be sat upon. Every object on display has a history, an association with a moment in the owners' lives.*

Because the painting isn't particularly interesting, it doesn't compete with the mosque. Instead, the painting becomes an arrow, a directional signal to make people look at the mosque.

The most intimate, personal displays are often layered ones of photos behind photos leaning against a wall. For example, in the front row there are intriguing mementos: a framed love letter from a grandfather to a grandmother alongside a spectacular seashell from Tahiti and an exquisite, tiny, ancient Roman glass bottle. Sometimes these displays are so layered that friends are afraid to touch them, because something might topple. Perhaps the implied message is do not touch. This is a visual diary, and you may have a glimpse, but secrets still prevail. Such displays of personal lives intrigue the viewer because they tell a social history—look at the clothes! the hairstyles!—and also reveal the characteristics of their owners. So if you embark upon a family tale, be prepared for intense scrutiny.

• Before putting something like this together, work on your visual instincts.

• Ask yourself whether the piece works within the wider concept.

• Place it onstage to see whether it works, leave it for a few days, then remove it. If there is a gap, put it back in; if not, leave it out.

RIGHT *A detail of some of the items displayed at the bottom of the bed, including an antique toilet set in a leather case, which belonged to a British Army officer. It sits on a cigar box made of porcupine quills.*

ABOVE *Plumb bobs (used in the building industry), snuff boxes, porcupine quill cigar boxes, and a toilet kit from an army officer are part of an eclectic collection displayed with panache. Dark leather collar boxes are on the left, and the round collar boxes on the right are wood. A turtle shell box on the left is a manicure set.*

A collection of boxes, mostly wooden, sits on an antique English sea chest. The white oval box is made of buffalo bone, another is of buffalo horn, another of leather, one of ivory, and the octagonal boxes have pewter lids. The larger box is Tunbridge. Some of these are from Morocco, India, and Italy. Two cups are from the Middle East, and the two lamp stands are turned in true Colonial style.

A smaller, lower table such as a coffee table can also have presence, depending on the material. If it is made of a slab of wood, metal, or stone, it has instant impact, and what is placed on it should be instantly enticing and have equal presence. Glass coffee table tops are a different matter. They are reflective, allowing delicate objects such as glass vases, to be seen in all their colorful glory. Light will play upon the form, too, at different times of the day.

Also, a coffee table is used everyday, so whatever you select to place upon its surface must be able to stand the touch of everyday admirers.

Consider using appropriate trays to display the objects designated for a tabletop. If you have a large table, and collections of only small things, place a tray on the table, and then put your objects into the tray, thus framing the collection. A tray could enhance a collection of silver bracelets, tiny thimbles, Victorian liqueur glasses, small carved Buddhas, or antique beaded evening bags. You could place a collection of nineteenth century Chinese porcelain tea cups on a lacquered tray so friends could hold the cups up to the light and see their opaque beauty.

LEFT *In a sunlit room, old wine flagons from Bordeaux, France sit on a solid wood chest used as a tabletop. There's a unique contrast in fragility and strength in that setting. Above the corner cupboard are old pots of confit d'oie. The settee is in the style of Louis XV and is covered in a Pierre Frey fabric.*

OPPOSITE *This tabletop is the focal point of a large and airy room with its three sculpted couplings. On the left is a bronze the owner found in a New Zealand antique store. The steel workers (seated) in the foreground were discovered in New York, and the third grouping is by the New Zealand artist Rick Rudd.*

This is a simple way to discover whether or not a piece of china is made of porcelain. If you cannot see through it, then it is made of another type of china and fired in a different way.

LARGE SURFACES

When you are fortunate enough to have a large table surface, one that can take grand objects, the matter of scale comes into play.

The photograph on the opposite page is a good example of this. The round table needs large objects to make an impact on its surface area.

Note that the tallest sculpture is placed in a central position, while each of the others claims its own space around it. The uniting theme is human figures. Though they are different in style and have been created by different artists, they have a secondary link that of sensuality.

It is present in the agile white figures, both leaning at precarious angles, thus creating an exhilarating tension in the work. It is especially apparent in the two bronze figures, both of whom are stretching in that sensual way that only a physical experience can bring about.

Sometimes the **unexpected table**
makes the small collection
more interesting—and provocative.

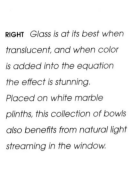

RIGHT *Glass is at its best when translucent, and when color is added into the equation the effect is stunning. Placed on white marble plinths, this collection of bowls also benefits from natural light streaming in the window.*

OPPOSITE *A collection of enamel pitchers ("brocs" in French) add a colorful note to a dark tabletop. Keeping them company is an ancient French dictionary. These items are clearly beloved.*

Why are they placed on different sides of the table, separated by the larger figure? They act as bookends to the central unit. Without this visual containment, the display would not be quite as successful. The result of the thoughful planning behind this display is impressive.

If you would like to emulate this type of display, remember it can work only in a large, airy room, presented as if it were in a gallery.

As you will have gathered by now, all it takes for an experienced collector to begin visualizing a tabletop display is to see an empty, flat surface. Within moments an avid collector will have a good idea of something they have tucked away in a cupboard that will suit the very space.

Once you have absorbed the information in this chapter you, too, will be able to look at a tabletop and begin to understand how a grouping of your personal treasures might look once in place on this island of space amid a sea of furniture.

COLOR

■ Think about how the color and texture of the container relates to and complements the collection. White ostrich eggs in a white ceramic container will not stand out, while placing the white eggs in a black container might look harsh. Maybe a large basket is the better solution.

LIGHT

■ Brilliantly colored glass marbles, mineral stones, and mercury balls may show up best when placed in a clear glass container that will reflect lots of light and beautifully enhance an object's transparency or sheen.

Silver Stories

LEFT *This collection of silver pill boxes would be lost if placed on the tabletop. When placed on a silver tray with other silver things, they present a united display.*

BELOW *Silver pieces sit comfortably with less important metallic pieces, walnut veneer obelisks, and a small box with pearl inlay strips. The roundness of the eggs, the nuts, and the lamp base provides a contrast to the sharp edges of the obelisks.*

Silver has been a precious metal for more than 5,000 years. When touched and handled over and over, it has a beautiful, subtle sheen.

The joy of collecting silver lies partly in its value, but mostly in its beauty. It does not have the flashiness of gold, nor the cold of stainless steel. Silver is passed down through generations and therefore has heirloom value.

In the sixteenth century, the French decorated silver objects with enamels and jewels while the English and Dutch embossed their silver with motifs of flowers and fruit. By the eighteenth century, America's best silversmiths were located in New York, Boston, and Philadelphia. Throughout Europe and America, silver had status. The wealthy displayed tureens and teapots, and hung silver labels that read "Port," "Sherry," "Claret" on crystal decanters.

The vocabulary of the silversmith is infinite, and the styles range from austere to ornate. Britain has attempted to control relatively pure silver by testing and marking it in the Goldsmith's Hall in the City of London. Other European countries have regulated the purity of silver, but not always consistently. Between 1881 and 1934, for example, Spanish silver had no quality controls at all. American silver may have the maker's mark, but little else.

Along with nearly pure silver, there is also silver plate, which is metal coated with silver. Items made of this are still collectible, but their value might be less.

ABOVE *Silver plates under the candles and the centrally placed silver lid with beaded handle contrast with the smooth dark timber surface of the console table in this office space. The painting is by New Zealand artist Gretchen Albrecht.*

LEFT *Small silver boxes are placed around a cylindrical silver vase, making it the focal point of a display placed under a large contemporary oil painting.*

Since the hearth is the **soul of any room**,
the mantel is the collection point.

On the Surface

Mantelpieces

*This pewter fireplace is home to an eclectic and personal collection of bits
and pieces placed in a regular line across the mantel.*

Since the hearth is the visual center, the source of heat and light in a room, the mantel is the natural place for display. People gaze at fires, mesmerized by the leap of flames, the sound of logs sputtering, and the flight of embers. So whatever you put on the mantel is guaranteed to be stared at intensely.

Mantels used to be the place where families displayed their crests, their ancient sabers, and their hunting trophies. What was above the mantel sometimes signified the family's status. Collections, such as those of rare porcelains, equally rare (even replicated!) Van Gogh paintings, or illuminated manuscripts signified wealth along with a passion for beautiful things.

But traditions are changing. In the nineteenth century, a clock or portrait might have gone on the mantel, flanked by a pair of vases. In the

twenty-first century, what goes on a mantel is less formal or predictable. The tick-tocking clock has been replaced by bottles, toys, and porcelain arranged somewhat wittily, and sometimes slightly asymmetrically. Now, symmetry is suggested, rather than strictly enforced. You no longer have to have matching pairs of candlesticks, portraits, or urns flanking a central object.

For a collector, that is a blessing, because pairs of anything—vases, Bohemian glass bottles, or oil lamps—not only cost more than a single item, but are also harder to find. You can now happily display treasures such as Art Deco pottery, and they do not have to be matched pairs.

Decorating a mantel today is more about what you like and consider in keeping with the style of the mantel than adhering to design rules. In this chapter, you will find intriguing relationships that will inspire you to think of your mantel as more than a place for a clock.

Unlike a tablescape, a mantel does not exist in architectural isolation. It is often part of a triptych, a center panel flanked by two walls. There is an architectural bilateral symmetry firmly in place. What a mantelpiece display should do is break up the static quality of the triptych by providing the eye with a worthwhile distraction.

Usually made of either fine timber (perhaps of smoothly worked oak, pine, redwood, or beech) or of marble, granite, and slate, a mantel is a sturdy structure. As such, it's an appealing place for display.

Like the tops of doors and cupboards, the mantel is a perfect place to put fragile, extraordinary, or expensive things. Cats can't reach mantels because they're too high; neither can rambunctious small children. However, a mantel is not like an isolated table, or a single horizontal plane. Every mantel's perpendicular expanse of wall is a perfectly natural place to hang a painting, a framed poster, or even a ship's figurehead. The choice is infinite and defined only by the physical boundaries of size and space. The display also connects to the wall opposite, particularly when mirrors are involved.

Everything has a link, corresponding **colors, shapes,** and **proportions.** These **three elements** go through all ages of design.

LEFT *In the tableau of ceramics, the plate is the focal point and is just slightly off-center, balanced (and contrasted with) the two vertical pieces. The grace notes, however, are the cinnamon-colored joss sticks. They break the symmetry and add a bolt of color.*

BELOW *A Parisian designer has Chinese blue and white ceramics and a small seashell; in a flamboyant move, he places a giant seashell on a table in front of the mantel. The shell is like a piece of sculpture, its curvilinear shape echoing that of the molding below the mantel.*

MIRRORS

You can hang or sit a mirror on or above the mantelpiece. But beware: A mirror reflects not just what's opposite it but an entire expanse of 180 degrees. It reflects perpendicular windows, curtains, walls, and air conditioners as well as what is outside a window, which could be an air shaft or a blinking neon sign. Before you commit to a large mirror, be sure that whatever is reflected is enticing. Mirrors are appealing when the view is altogether pleasing, and when the objects on the mantelpiece are three-dimensional and can be perceived in the round. These things can include

busts, vases, candleholders, toys, pitchers, plates, and evocative seashells.

When selecting a mirror, think carefully about the frame. Is its design in harmony with the other decorative items in the room? Will the frame be heavy and upset the delicate balance of furniture, soft furnishings, and other accessories? If you love the idea of a moulded and gilt-framed fancy mirror or a hand-crafted country-style twig frame, yet do not have furniture to match, it might not be suitable. The same concern applies to the width of the mirror frame. A large frame that is quite wide and of dark wood might not suit a smaller room. Think about proportions and the impact of color and design before making your decision.

HEARTH WITHOUT A MANTEL

Not all hearths have mantels. Modern hearths are often placed within a flat wall that soars from floor to ceiling. That does not mean you cannot display things. The space above leaping flames is still available for display. You can hang textural

ABOVE *A London antiquities dealer placed a Joseph Gott sculpture of an unknown woman on the mantel and surrounded it with Wedgwood creamware, terra-cotta pots and vases. What commands attention is the woman.*

OPPOSITE *A collector found the terra-cotta tiles that form the bas relief columns and commissioned a ceramicist to make matching crackle glaze tiles for the fireplace. A nineteenth century cast-iron shooting target sits teasingly on the mantel. Dragons frame the fireplace tools and above is a lithograph of an indoor New York ice skating rink.*

items such as Amish quilts, antique flags, and an ancestor's portrait above the hearth, imagining an horizontal line that would have been the mantel.

Figure out the proportion by holding things above the hearth, until you feel it looks right. Something that seems to easily fit into the space rather than loom large and take over the space, is preferable. In the case of portraits and other paintings, a single item is preferable to several.

If you feel you do not have the confident eye of a professional, look through books and magazines and take note of the way objects are arranged on a mantel, large with small, lots with a few. The general rule is for taller and larger items to go behind smaller, wider items so each can be fully seen. Experiment with objects of different sizes, placing them next to one another, in front and behind, leaving space among the objects, until you think the arrangement looks right.

You can take a flat wall surrounding a hearth, and build a mantel onto the wall. (Perhaps contact an architect to help you design it.) If the existing architecture is modern and minimalist, you will

Collections have a **presence**. They **communicate** with your environment.

OPPOSITE *The owner of this display played directly to the symmetry of the room. Primavera pots alternate in size and shape along the mantel as well as on the consoles in front of the radiators. A Venetian mirror reflects the picture on the opposite wall, and in front of the fireplace there is more Primavera but not pots. Isadora Duncan is swirling on the table. Cast-iron griffins flank the fireplace.*

want a mantel that is similar in style. What you put on it, however, can be from any era. You could place a prancing Tang dynasty horse, a seventeenth century map (a bold one so it is visible), or even a taxidermist's specimen of a white owl there.

Some mantelpieces are of a design associated with a distinct era, for example, Art Nouveau, Victorian, or Rococo. However, you are not bound to display objects of that era. You may, of course, but you do not have to. Just as tables can be juxtaposed with the collection on top so can mantelpieces. If you want to experiment with eclectic touches, look for a unifying element between the mantel and the items, be it color, texture, or form. That way, you can ensure the assemblage will work.

RULES OF DISPLAY

When you have more than one object on a mantel (real or imagined), they must connect to each other. Christian Duc, a designer based in Paris, collects Vietnamese and Chinese artifacts. His well-defined rules of display apply to every kind of collection imaginable.

Whatever you might be grouping, find the unifying element. Should you choose brown as the color theme for ceramics, then other shades of brown might visually connect a Japanese wood chest to paler and darker ceramics nearby. Work around the dominant color.

TEN GREAT MANTEL ITEMS

- ■ elegantly framed mirror

- ■ distinctive vase

- ■ clock

- ■ antique ceramic sculpture

- ■ small marble bust

- ■ framed painting or sketch

- ■ distinctive figurine

- ■ handmade beaten silver bowl

- ■ impressive decorative china plate

ABOVE *Columns and golden brickwork combined with solemn figures bring a classical theme to this display. The framed book behind the ornaments is a deft touch.*

OPPOSITE *Here is a view of the mantel from afar. You can see it is a combination of items, but all have a classical theme or shape; hence, the whole display works.*

Color as connective tissue works in any kind of collection, precious or homely. You can display only Venetian glass goblets, which are of different colors but are unified by their extraordinary curvy shapes that include spiraling stems. Another example—Native American fat black pots could work on a mantel, unified by color alone, not by maker or form.

What flanks a mantel is as important as what is on the mantel. Balance is key. Sometimes a room or a collection dictates a symmetrical design. A living room had a hearth flanked by two walls, each of which had a radiator. Clearly symmetry was in order. The owner placed terra-cotta on the mantelpiece, and to hide the radiators, displayed more terra-cotta on consoles placed in front of the radiators. To encourage the eye to look up, the owner hung a mirror over the mantel and two vertical paintings above the consoles.

Sometimes symmetry is not required, and two disparate collections can be displayed on either side of the mantel. What is then required is lots of space between the mantel and the collections. You do not want them to compete any more than you do when you place a display on adjacent walls. Either displays talk to each other, or they should be far enough away to stand on their own.

Inexpensive objects can look equally interesting on a mantel. Enter the foyer of a home belonging to two New York art directors and guess what greets you? A quartet of paper shirts displayed above a mantel flanked by a collection of globes (not the type that turn into a cocktail cabinet). The colorful shirts are Chinese funeral offerings,

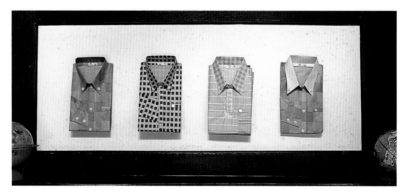

LEFT *This entrance foyer has four paper shirts lined up above the mantel. They are Chinese funeral offerings, but in this context, they signify fashion, ephemera, and surprise.*

ABOVE *The four paper shirts cost a few dollars each and were found at Mee Lun, a shop in Manhattan's Chinatown, which also sells paper televisions, beer cans, and running shoes.*

RIGHT *This living room has eye-popping symmetry. Six large cast iron Coke bottles are from the fence of a coke bottling plant, and are dated 1933. A pair of carved wood kewpie dolls, from 1940s ice cream trucks, perch on custom-made shelves.*

A mantel, whether **real** or **imagined**, is the
bottom part of a picture frame.

cost only a few dollars each, and delight by surprise. They are fashion. They are ritual.

They were also the solution to the question of what to put in this entrance. The couple considered words, like HOME, with a frame around it, but dismissed that as banal. They also thought of a Rockwell Kent lithograph, but dismissed that as somber. Both understood that a collection reveals the personality of the collector, and banal and somber was not how the couple wanted to be seen. The current display reveals their quirky style.

Or a mantel can simply be left bare, and the one significant possession you want to display, for example, an Andy Warhol silk screen, an Indian feather headdress, or a nineteenth century silk kimono, can simply hang above.

A mantel does not have to have anything on it, but it is enhanced by additional material.

RIGHT *In this living room, a coffee table is left usefully bare, except for flowers. Other surfaces have been carefully curated. To the right of the fireplace, a curio cabinet holds miniature chairs. The top of the inglenook holds books published by Insel Verlag on artists such as Goya, Klee, and Matisse.*

RIGHT *Ingenious charm, animation, geometric silhouettes and an absolute total lack of realism unite this parade of toys. Tom Nussbaum made the tin knife over the mantelpiece, which the owner sees as a spoof of the baronial ancestral sabers and rifles.*

Revisit your collection from time to time
to rearrange it and rotate pieces in or out.

RIGHT *Colorful and stylish Art Deco pottery can add visual interest to any shelf or alcove. Sometimes pieces found at flea markets are suitable; other moments require pedigree and only the work of Clarice Cliff will suffice.*

BELOW *Blue and white pottery has been the inspiration for many a kitchen hutch display. Here, a mix of makers, styles, and forms creates a charming domestic scene.*

The Chinese kept the art of porcelain-making secret from Europe until 1709, when it was first made in Meissen, Germany, before spreading to other European cities.

Porcelain, then, was a luxurious material. In China, porcelain-makers signed with the name of an Emperor, and often the period it was made. In Europe, factories such as the Medici Porcelain Factory, Meissen, and J. Wedgwood, all marked their wares. Forgery of marks, however, is not uncommon.

Thin, sometimes translucent, porcelain was not the only type of art pottery. By the end of the nineteenth century, the more common earthenware pots, jars, and vases became collectible.

Americans came somewhat late to art pottery. Various international expositions inspired the birth of Rookwood Pottery of Cincinnati in 1880. Charles Fergus Binns (1857–1934), an Englishman, moved to America, where he taught students how to unify form and glaze. William Victor Bragdon (California Faience) and Paul Cox (Newcomb Pottery) learned from him. In Mississippi, George Ohr (1857–1918), made earthenware as thin as eggshell porcelain, twisted, folded, and crushed into pitchers, vases, and bowls, and hats, animal heads and potatoes. He kept thousands of pieces for himself, and predicted that they would someday be worth their weight in gold. They sell for hundreds of dollars up to more than $5,000.

He may have been right.

Art Pottery

RIGHT *Black and white forms sit in relief against a white background, framed by a chic unit of shelves. These act as a room divider, and what better way of turning them into a focal point than placing single pots in each square, repeating the forms in a casual pattern.*

BELOW *A color theme of red and white (or cream) was decided upon by the owners of this neat kitchen hutch. A careful selection of the shape of these useful objects unites them in a glorious way.*

Take steps to display your **prized possessions** so that they can be seen in all their **beauty**.

Support
Acts
Shelves

Here, a wall of open shelving units acts as a divider between the end of the dining room and the stairs leading down to another level. The objects are moved around at the owners' pleasure.

Unlike a mantel or a table, a shelf is a somewhat anonymous, supporting piece of design. While it does not have the decorative importance of other domestic furniture, the finest shelf plays an important role in the art of display, albeit a supporting role, almost vanishing into the background, allowing the objects to leap into focus, to be center stage.

Shelves, by their anonymity, are appealing when least expected. Take the niches in staircases in nineteenth century town houses on the East Coast. They are sometimes called "coffin corners" because when someone died in an upstairs bedroom, the undertakers took a coffin up the narrow staircase, turning it in the corner niche so that they could easily take it all the way to the top and down again. Those niches, which usually feature a single shelf, are perfect settings for an object that can be viewed in splendid isolation as you ascend the stairs, pausing to enjoy its beauty.

Shelves can be installed in the most unexpected places. For example, one homeowner created shelves in his white-tiled bathroom out of four blocks of cobalt blue glass. On each was a personal treasure including a framed collection of butterflies and a bowl of fossils from Wyoming and Montana.

The humble shelf is more than somewhere to put clocks or towels; it can be a work of art. It can be hard-edged, made of sophisticated brushed stainless steel, with either end turning up to become bookends. It can be smooth with rounded edges, its form undulating across a blank wall; or an artisan's quirky free-standing shelf unit created from tropical wood, with shelves in differing shapes and sizes and placed at all angles, as shown at the recent furniture show in Milan. Whatever your taste, be it a pile of 1970s retro metal and glass cubes; a chic, modern modular design; or shelves made of ancient French pine; you will find a shelf style to suit your taste here.

Where do you put a favorite collectible, be it a Venetian handkerchief glass bowl, a papier-mâché mask, or a bronze Buddha? Do you place it on a shelf that makes it visible, tactile, and easily picked up yet also vulnerable to dust, people stomping about, and the occasional earthquake? Or do you put it in the safekeeping of a cabinet (which still doesn't prevent it tumbling out during an earthquake)?

The answer depends on how you like to display your favorite things, the size of the objects, your desire to have them visible twenty-four hours a day, the object's affinity for attracting dust and your willingness to either hire someone to dust them or to dust the collection yourself.

Like walls and tables, shelves are on display day and night and are visible from every angle. Some collectors may rotate their collections in order to

BELOW *A minimalist black granite unit lit from three recessed lights. On the top shelf, left to right, a 1940s bird carved out of limestone, a woman's head made by a ship's chandler, and a terra-cotta man. In the niche, lights focus on a large weathervane.*

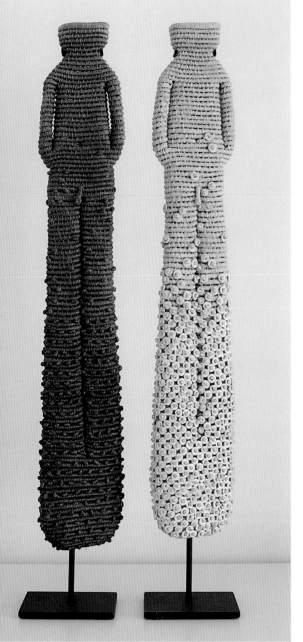

LEFT *Shelves are set within walls to display these two figures by Mary Giles next to each other. They are called "Artifact Pair" and are made from waxed linen. Together, they appear to be waiting for something to happen.*

ABOVE *Every twig and every peg in the basket by John McQueen, called "Red Osier Twig Basket" aims to give a good impression of a porcupine. The basket made with pussy willows is by Markku Kosonen. Both stand out in relief against the pristine white walls.*

BELOW *A ceramic landscape bowl entitled "Mirage Canyon Winter" (1986) is highly textured inside and out, and the zigzag pattern that represents a meandering river, swirls up from the base. Because the shelf is built into the wall, it seems to disappear, leaving you face to face with the pot.*

show each piece off at various times of the year; however, a shelf really is for something you want to see constantly, pick up, and handle.

For some people, there is also the notion that unless an object is visible it is of no use and might as well not exist. For them, the visible objects, whether antique globes, duck decoys, or African American memorabilia are a source of reflection and are imbued with memories. They are also an inspiring source of new ideas.

Size and material help determine whether or not a collection of objects will be best displayed

ABOVE *This large open shelf has several functions. It allows objects to be seen in the round; it lets light through from one room to another, and it acts as part of a room divider.*

on a shelf, in a cabinet, or in a glass cabinet. Tiny domestic things such as buttons and cufflinks, scrimshaw, and arrow tips are lost when placed on a shelf. They are better seen all together, framed and hung on a wall, put on a small table in a clever configuration, or placed in a small glass cabinet.

Fragile paper objects—paper sculpture, art books, papier-mâché masks—can get dusty, and eventually look irretrievably worn and tattered. So can delicate textiles, such as antique lace collars, Chinese silk badges, and embroidered silk evening bags. Larger, sturdier things, however, such

The **weight of the object** dictates
the thickness and span of the shelf.

LEFT *These shelves are picture rails inserted seamlessly into the wall. Each shelf has a three-quarter-inch lip, so that the photos won't slip off the shelves. Since the picture frames are not identical, there's a casualness to this display.*

as pitchers, Japanese baskets, and scholar's rocks, can live happily on shelves.

Shelves, by the way, do not have to be built against a wall. They can be cleverly designed as a free-standing unit and be open on both sides. You can put them in the middle of a room so they act as a divider, and then you can see your millefiori glass paperweights, green Depression glassware, or cobalt stoneware crocks from both sides.

This use of shelving units can be useful if a room is smaller in size and tends to be dark. In this situation, open shelves let light through to the far side of a room. Their design ought to be of a solid construction, not lightweight, especially if the unit is designed for a high traffic area of a room.

ABOVE *A circular wall is filled with shelves of books within easy reach of anyone sitting on the plush sectional sofa. Vases and other decorative items are interspersed with books to break up the density.*

SHELF SIZE

There are three things to consider when you are looking at shelves: thickness, depth, and height. When you build shelves, ask yourself whether the collection is complete or is just beginning. Perhaps you have just started to collect Japanese lacquerware. Have you a dozen pieces, say cups and bowls, all of similar sizes, or are they of very different sizes and shapes? Do they include boxes and trays? Is this the complete collection, or can you see this passion for Japanese wares expanding to include vertical hand-drums? And later, perhaps warrior helmets embellished with spikes?

Think about a six-inch cube versus a six-inch needle thin object, or a six-inch bar, lying on its side, and think about what's next to it.

If you have a six-inch-high thin object, you might need a tall and thin niche or a square one. And if you have a low and flat six-inch-long object, you might want a very high niche which would point out the flatness of the object, or you could design a long and wide niche which would mimic the object. The issue is context.

If you had a Giacometti sculpture, and you put it in a tiny niche, you will make it look trapped. If you sat it on a pedestal with a lot of air around it, it could look alienated. Or, conversely, an object can sometimes be placed in a confining space, and look as though it is ready to burst, and therefore it seems to have more power, more presence, and more energy attached to it.

What you collect clearly determines the height, depth, and thickness of your shelves which an architect or interior designer should design for you. If you prefer to make the shelves yourself, consult a friendly builder or handyman before you start putting them in place.

The weight of the object and its neighbors will dictate the thickness and span of the shelf. Your collection also dictates whether or not you should have permanent fixed shelves or adjustable ones. The latter are best when a collection is in flux. Most people choose adjustable shelving knowing that the support system is visible.

When shelves are supported by pegs inserted into holes, architects can have indentations made in the shelves so that the pegs slip into these indentations and are flush with the bottom of the shelves. The holes on the sides of the system, however, can't be disguised. Either you can attempt to ignore them or have the architect drill more holes so that they become part of a patttern on the sides of the shelving system.

LEFT *Chosen for their brilliant red color, these vases are also in various shapes and sizes. Despite the difference in shape and form, they make a solid collection.*

BELOW *Shelves are built to fit above a doorway leading to a dining room in this home. The owners reveal their penchant for books, magazine, and pottery through the various groupings on the shelves. It shows an excellent use of space.*

LEFT *Architects designed this metal system, bolting the shelf and rods into the walls so they cannot topple over. Each shelf is sixteen-inches-high, tall enough for books and other collections. The bookcases are backlit with lights placed on a plexiglass shelf and behind on a molding. The library ladder gives access to top shelves.*

RIGHT *The owner collects masks from Africa, New Guinea, Mexico, and other countries because he loves their expressiveness. He rotates the masks, keeping some in storage and others on display on the bookcases in his study. Each mask has ample room so it can be examined closely.*

BOOKSHELVES

Books, whether rare first editions or everyday volumes, are popular collectibles. Not all books, however, are so visually enticing as to be worthy of display. Random paperbacks, for example, an Agatha Christie placed next to a Stephen King and a battered copy of the *Grapes of Wrath* tend to look untidy on bookcases. Even a paperback copy of *The Complete Works of Shakespeare* can look a little tired after a few years. Covers get torn and pages turn yellow.

However, if you have a complete collection of Penguin paperbacks in mint condition, and you neatly arrange them in alphabetical order by author, that is a different matter.

Generally speaking though, books that are considered light vacation reading can be squirreled away behind closed doors or passed on to friends and other travelers.

What to do with precious magazines? An entire collection of magazines—for instance, copies of *Vogue*, *National Geographic*, or *The Economist* from January 1950 to now—can look quite appealing if the magazines are lined up vertically, or placed in neat horizontal stacks. Be sure to have thick shelving for such magazine collections because they are extremely heavy, and lesser shelves have been known to bend from the sheer weight of the volumes.

Here is a passing observation: A large collection of the same thing implies some depth on the collector's part, or at least a single strand of obsession!

Good-looking hardcover books, however, suggest a permanence and a stimulating visual presence. Decide how you want to display them—vertically, horizontally, or both. Placing books vertically means the shelves must be the right height to take a variety of sizes. Place them so the title printed on the spine is easily read. Do not squash books into a space. They need room to breathe.

ABOVE *This collection of African masks is displayed either on telescopic stands or are attached to the wall. The masks reveal intense emotions and are arranged so that there is a certain empathy between them.*

RIGHT *"Fame," an 1885 weathervane depicting an angel needed air, a free-standing space, and a place to soar. It found a home on this railing and was screwed into the post as a safety precaution.*

However, letting them rest at an angle is also bad for them because the spine can collapse.

Oversized, lavish coffee-table books can easily be damaged, so measure the height of the tallest and design the shelves to incorporate these expensive investments. Cramming them causes the jacket to rip, and the hardcover itself to wear down and this can affect the future resale value.

Some books always lean over when they are on the end of a row. In this situation bookends are essential, but if you do not have a pair place three or four books on top of each other horizontally to act as a book end.

To keep the eye traveling across the shelves, intersperse books with a framed photograph or two, a sculpture, or a vase filled with fresh flowers. Some people put photos directly in front of books. If you never plan to read the books that's fine. However, if you want to refer to them, putting things in front of books is impractical. Stacking books on the sides of a staircase is an attractive display or storage solution if you've run out of shelf space, but keep in mind that the books may become soiled or damaged in such an exposed location.

Shelving is the staple of a storage
system in any room.

LEFT *A juxtaposition of the old and the new exists here on a gleaming granite kitchen bench. The small figure on a stand is solemn, its face full of ancient wisdom.*

RIGHT *A weathervane depicting an Indian about to shoot an arrow perches on the range hood. The positioning is clever. The high perch gives the weathervane drama.*

OPPOSITE *Some people display cookie jars on the kitchen counter. Here, however, a small sculpture is displayed on the counter surface.*

THE ODD SHELF

A shelf doesn't have to be part of a larger system. It can be a lone horizontal plane that naturally lends itself as a surface for display, such as the hood of a range (see photo opposite), a single shelf built out from a wall, a stair railing, or a picture rail along the wall in a hallway. It can be a piece of newly sanded, painted wood supported by two ornamental wrought iron brackets that were flea market finds. It can be a French baker's rack, metal shelving once used in a supermarket, or a pile of beat-up suitcases stacked horizontally. Whatever you use, an odd shelf can be effective as a point of display in a room where shelf space is at a premium.

The top of a row of kitchen cabinets is not strictly a shelf but it provides a good place for display. Objects do no have to be associated with food, cooking, or eating—the African mask seen here looks at home. Art is omnipresent.

READY-MADE SHELVES

There is a wide range of ready-made shelving units available from furniture companies such as Ikea. You will find there are designs available for just about everything including books, figurines, ceramic bowls, and glass vases. There is also a choice of free-standing shelves or those that can be fitted to a wall. The range of widths, lengths, and finishes of both the shelf and its support (if needed) is excellent. Clear instructions and screws come with each purchase so they are not that difficult to construct.

Ready-made shelves can be made of a variety of materials, including steel, aluminium, wood and medium density fiberboard which is usually covered with a veneer, making it able to take more weight than some natural timber shelves. If you want the shelves to last a few years, it is preferable to go for quality over price because then at least

you have the possibility of the veneer staying attached to the fiberboard longer. If you don't like the veneer, but the shelf is perfect in other ways, you can disguise it with another finish.

Self-assembled cubes can be used to create lots of different shapes and to fill awkward corners with an attractive assemblage. Clutter can be hidden behind a cupboard door while more attractive objects can be displayed in their own space. The flexibility of cubes is appealing, especially since they can easily be moved around the room.

Consider industrial shelving units for display. These create a high-tech look and can conflict with the existing decorative style if you are not careful, but it is definitely worth looking at designs the commercial suppliers have to offer.

Things you would not usually consider can make a contribution as display shelves in the broadest sense, including plastic racks and wire baskets.

LEFT *This intriguing kitchen tableau has clock-plates hanging on the wall above a suspended glass shelf. "A Stitch in Time Saves Nine" reads one of the clocks. There's a multiplicity of shapes here grouped like with like.*

RIGHT *A simple yet highly effective display is this one of glazed ceramics organized by color. Since the shelves are transparent, light pours through and makes the ceramics look particularly vivid.*

BELOW *The pottery teapot and matching cups are Japanese and the creamer is Czechoslovakian. They are related to each other by their perky little faces.*

PERMANENT SHELVING

Permanent, custom-built shelving works for those whose collections are intact. The sleekest shelves are those which are inserted into a horizontal recess designed to fit the shelves. The support system is invisible, and the shelf appears to be a seamless part of the wall.

Hand-built shelves have obvious advantages. The choice of basic materials is wider than when selecting from ready-made units; you can be sure they will fit your allocated space and they can be made to match the existing decorative scheme of your home. Using professional cabinetmakers can be expensive, so it is best to obtain more than one quote when putting the work out to estimate. Doing it yourself is cheaper, but you have to consider how well you will do it, and whether you have the time to spend on the task.

SHELF MATERIAL

- When deciding what type of shelf, you need to ask these questions.
  - Should the shelf be transparent, translucent, or opaque?
  - Should it be made of clear, sand-blasted, or etched glass?
  - Should it be made of wood and if so, what kind of wood? Oak, pine, ash, or mahogany?
  - Can it be made of steel or perforated steel? Should it be painted white, like the walls?

- When shelves are glass, they have to be dusted regularly. On the other hand, the more transparent the shelves, the easier they are to light, because light goes through them.

ABOVE *A frosted glass wall separates the library from the master bathroom allowing light to go into the bathroom. The bookcases hold, besides books, a selection of photographs and personal objects from around the world.*

RIGHT *Glass shelves hold all of the drinking paraphernalia needed to make perfect cocktails. Glass decanters, silver and stainless steel shakers, and a tray laid with glasses are ready for guests.*

BELOW *This bright, open-plan kitchen has a simple but textured cabinet system. Some shelves are for open display, with groupings of like with like, for example, glass with glass, metal with metal. Neatness, order, and variety count in all the displays.*

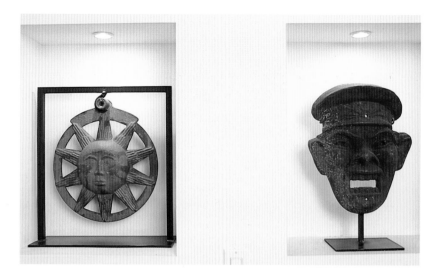

LIGHTING

Before you light your shelved collection, consider which pieces you want to bring into focus. Is it the face of a mask? The irridescent pinks, yellows, and blues of a hand-blown glass bowl? Or the texture of a hand-thrown pottery vase? Having come to a conclusion, you must then consider how to achieve the right ambience.

For sculpture, you light from above with the light aimed toward the front. Track lighting may be commonplace, but it works in this situation. For items made of glass, back-lighting is beautiful and effective.

For translucent shadow puppets, back-lighting can also be effective. You can install light in the back of the cabinet and cover the source of light with milk plexiglass, or translucent glass.

To focus on a texture, for example, in the case of a horizontally ridged vase, you light from the top, which is against the grain. It creates more shadow. If a vase has vertical ribs, light it from the side. Do not light an object from all directions, because then the lighting becomes flat and bland.

Always place a light to accent the piece as a focal point. If you place light beneath a shelf to shine on what is below, it also has the effect of making the shelf appear to float.

ABOVE *In the left niche sits a nineteenth century cast iron trade sign for an insurance company, made in the shape of a sun. At right is a cast iron shooting gallery target in the form of Emperor Hirohito. These two objects are united by their rough material.*

RIGHT AND OPPOSITE *Three interesting pieces of pottery by a Californian potter, Jeffrey A. Zigulis, are displayed on a single shelf with the tallest piece in the center becoming the focal point of the trio. The curlicues of the brackets echo the curlicues of the chair below.*

TYPES OF LIGHT

Low-wattage incandescent light casts a soft, warm, even light and is the solution for any collection where color is important, for example, when shining on textiles, paintings, and sculpture.

Tungsten halogen offers a sparklier, colder light and produces high-contrast shadows. It might

work well with a collection of faceted jewels, a glass vase, or a collection of cut-crystal glassware. Light will reflect brightly and enhance the beauty of each piece.

Overhead lights can cause problems, especially when a beam comes down steeply, since it can create ugly vertical shadows that will draw the eye away from the object you want to focus on. Use antiglare devices, such as reflectors or rims, attached to fittings to give directional light. Or, add warm reflectors on spots to soften the effect.

Whichever type of light you use, put the light on a dimmer so you can manipulate the ambience to produce your own special effects light show. For instance, for a dinner party you may want to place lots of candles on the dining table, then dim many of the surrounding lights.

Then, turn up the lights aimed at a spectacular collection of Venetian glass goblets where the rims unfurl like blossoms, and the stems spiral and splay out into a delicate filigreed base. You are limited only by your imagination.

LEFT *In this dining room, a collection of French and American pitchers and crocks are sweetly displayed on racks. On the top shelf the tallest pitcher is the obvious focal point, flanked by two smaller ones.*

PITCHERS

French baker's shelves and pitchers go together like love and marriage, as you can see from these photographs. Handsome and sculptural, pitchers are at home in the kitchen and love to be seen on display. Pitchers come in many different shapes and sizes, are decorated or plain, and all of them feature elegant pourers and endearing handles.

Not sure which type to collect? You can decide to collect only miniatures, French Art Deco styles, pitchers of a single color or pattern, oversize types, transferware, or Victorian molded designs. Ewers (pitchers with long necks) are also collectible. You might be taken by a fluted pourer, the embossing, or its bulbous shape. In a short time, you will find you have amassed a collection spanning several centuries and different styles.

Displaying pitchers is made easier by their form and dignity. Place three or four of different sizes in a row, handles facing the same way, and you will have created an admirable group.

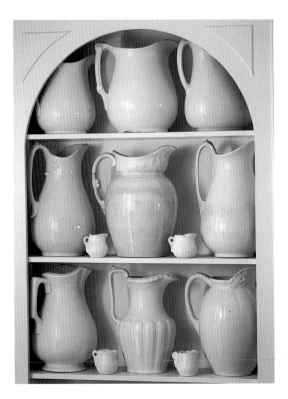

LEFT *The collection of pitchers and crocks stands out because of the sunshine beaming in on the domestic enamelware and pottery. On the two top shelves, the tallest object is in the center. One pitcher sits in solitary splendor on a chair which, if not needed for seating, is an obvious shelf. Bottles sit on the window sill, and light amplifies the colors of the bottles.*

RIGHT *These pitchers, all facing the same direction, are happily crowded into a cupboard, and somehow their voluptuous shapes seem to be even more exaggerated by being so close together. Tiny pitchers are a sweet juxtaposition in scale to the big pitchers.*

Whatever material pitchers are made from, they contain a certain poise, a stillness before movement—that of pouring liquids.

Early nineteenth century pitchers were made in taupe, tan, and beige as well as white, cream, and creamy gray. Some have smooth, glazed surfaces; others are designed with trims around fluted lips or are patterned on the main body. When you look closely at a pitcher with an allover pattern, you will see the pattern was molded into the clay.

For those who admire ornate vases, search out antique Wedgwood pitchers with twisted handles and bodies decorated with grapevines and heroic and mythological figures.

Salt glaze pitchers, made since the 1700s, have a gray-white, slightly pitted surface. Spatterware, or spongeware pitchers in colors such as blue, green, and red also date from the eighteenth century. Tiny white syrup pitchers can be found at flea markets for ten dollars. Always pick a pitcher up by its bowl; handles break off easily.

LEFT *These shelves tell a picturesque story of a life well-lived, of journeys undertaken. Photographs and prints are stacked in front of one another in an orderly way. Although the shelves are busy, they are not cluttered.*

RIGHT *The shelves are permanent, since they slip into the walls, but because the heights of the shelves vary so much, there is flexibility for display.*

THE PICTURE RAIL

Picture rails are friendly gestures. They invite people to pick up the photos and examine them. Although a picture rail is defined as the molding from which a picture is hung, it can simply be a shallow horizontal shelf or a series of shelves. It can run as a solitary horizontal line across a wall or the length of a hallway.

What makes a picture rail useful is its raised lip which can measure about one to two inches. It becomes a perfect place to display photographs and small framed prints. The rail's lip prevents photographs from slipping off.

If you do not already have a picture rail with a wide lip, then attach a section of moulding to your wall. The length of a new picture rail should be based on how many pictures you want to display. There are other considerations: do you want one picture placed behind the other, and how much

room do you have for the rail? Is it going to be attached to a huge living room wall where there is lots of empty space, or will the rail be placed on a wall in a narrow corridor? In the case of the latter, it shouldn't jut out too many inches.

Once you have answered those questions, choose a molding to suit the style of the rest of the space and one with the strength to hold both the picture frames and the glass. If the space is Art Deco, then find a length of Art Deco molding; if minimalist in style, select a simple molding and use minimalist frames. Perhaps frame all the images with the same type of frame.

If you have a lot of pictures and a long stretch to fill, measure the width of each frame, find the total length if you placed them end to end, then check that they will fit on the molding. If they do not all fit, decide which you will leave out of the display, and then find a home for these elsewhere.

Perfume bottles are like jewels
gleaming in a cluster around a spartan
white bath, promising pleasure.

GROUPING ON SHELVES

The same rules apply to grouping things on shelves as on walls, tables, and mantels. You are telling a visual story, marrying like to like, and looking for a variety of textures and silhouettes, heights, and depths. The perfume bottles on two shelves by the small window, opposite, are arranged like with like, and by shape and size. Tall bottles are at the back of the shelf, and the bottles are then placed close together. Most of the caps are of Bakelite, which makes the display more interesting. The bottles directly surrounding the bath are within arm's reach, ready to use.

If the items to be displayed are different, look for a common thread. This could be a color, a form, or a texture. Or each object could be made by the same company or artist, as in a collection of ceramic bowls ranging in time from the very first to the most recent example of the potter's work. In the latter case, the collection tells a story.

Placing objects in groups of three or four works well on shelves, or if you have a long shelf, you could place groups of two, then single, objects along the shelf as seen on the previous page where the selected pieces have a similar look, yet they are from entirely different eras.

ABOVE *A series of tiny shells, all by themselves, would be boring. What appeals in this grouping is the dominance of the big shell which, by implication, makes the little ones more intriguing.*

LEFT *In this bathroom, a collection of perfume, cologne, and lotion bottles, all made between 1910 and 1950, are grouped around the tub and on shelves. The bathroom is the perfect room for the bottles.*

Fixed-height shelves present fixed perameters. Look at the proportion of an object before deciding where it should go. Individual objects need space top and bottom, left and right. Placing them at the back of a shelf hides them from view, so go for middle to front each time.

GLASS SHELVES

To hold the load of so many bottles, as seen on the opposite page, glass shelves must be thick and shatter-proof, and the supports must be able to take the weight, too.

Glass shelves are also perfect for the beauty of shells, whether large or small. The image on this page shows one large shell as the focal point of a much larger display that takes up several shelves. If you were to place these shells on a solid wood shelf, either painted white or left natural, the display would lose some of its fragility. Plus, the luminosity that occurs when the light is at various angles during the day, highlighting some shells and throwing others into shadow, would be lost. Standing each shell on its end required patience, however, the final result is effective and gives the viewer a better idea of their form and coloring than had they been laid on their sides.

Alcoves

RIGHT *In this tiny alcove each small group of objects is centered, and the tallest object becomes the central focal point. The muted colors and the warm tones of the cabinet are harmonious.*

LEFT *Against a colored grid, solid-color objects are displayed and thus demand attention. Patterned objects or intricately shaped objects would disappear against the background.*

OPPOSITE *This alcove was once a doorway. Because the owner required more shelves, he had it converted to a simple alcove fitted with glass shelves. Here, he displays a collection of antique Chinese ceramic bowls, plates, and vases against a white background,*

Alcoves are surprising places to insert a few essential shelves when you need space for display. They are like sliver buildings in an urban landscape. They're recessed and faintly awkward spaces which make them all the more appealing. You'll find them in traditional Colonial houses where space was at a premium, and the desire to display treasures was strong enough to find a solution.

Alcoves can be found anywhere, in bathrooms, hallways, living rooms, and in kitchens. They are often unused space next to a structural wall, door, or pipe. Precisely because they are spaces that are too small for furniture, they can be outfitted to display private collections.

If the alcove is tall and narrow, you might want to insert glass shelves so you can light it just from the top and let the light filter through to the bottom shelf. The narrower the shelves and the smaller the alcove, the more stark the display might seem and it needs light to enhance objects placed there. To make things stand out, group them in a simple way.

An alcove is ideal for young, undeveloped collections because the initial few items you buy will not look lost and as the collection grows, you can move objects around until they are at rest.

Cabinets are perfect for the kinds
of things you want to have around but
don't want to endanger.

Behind Closed

Doors

Cabinets

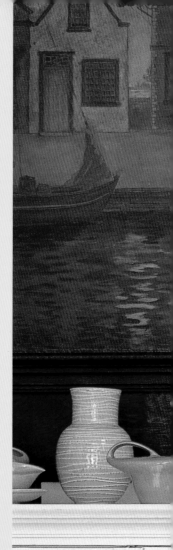

Domestic pottery is safely housed in a glass-fronted cabinet. It can be seen, yet is
untouchable by sticky fingers. The top of the cabinet is used as a shelf and chic treasures
have been placed here.

C abinets possess mystery. Recently, a friend opened the translucent doors of her refrigerator to reveal a modern domestic still-life. Because she could see the silhouettes of whatever was within, she had arranged the contents of her refrigerator like art. Milk was in a cobalt blue pitcher. Orange juice was in a red ceramic pitcher. The two pitchers, which did not match but were of the same 1940s era, faced each other. Butter was in a sparkling glass dish. The food was treated like jewelry and the refrigerator as a cabinet.

When the contents of a cabinet, whether it is food in a refrigerator or sparkling emeralds in a jeweler's display case, are arranged with an eye to presentation, they become that much more interesting. Another friend arranges all her dishes in her kitchen cabinets by color. One shelf is devoted entirely to earthy terra-cotta dishes from Chile, Spain,

Korea, Ireland, and Haiti. They speak to her of food from those lands, of rice and beans, of paellas; when she looks at them, they inspire her to cook.

Thus, a cabinet in a domestic situation can be a great source of inspiration. It is no small wonder that the gleaming cocktail cabinet became so fashionable in the 1960s and 1970s, because you knew what was waiting inside—smart silver cocktail sets that suggested Bloody Marys, Manhattans, and classic martinis. Reflecting in the mirror were those twinkling crystal glasses just asking to be filled with a spirited liquid.

In this chapter, you will find cabinets of different eras, shapes, and styles. Each belongs to an individual who cares passionately about whatever it is he or she collects. However, they all have one thing in common. Their cabinets are full of curiosities.

The great phrase,"cabinet of curiosities" comes from the Renaissance era but is applicable today. For what is a cabinet that is full of Korean celadon cups, green Depression glassware, or a few bits of African American memorabilia but a cabinet that reflects your curiosity?

This tradition began in the Renaissance in sixteenth century Italy, and spread throughout Europe. The Renaissance was the era when the power, creativity, and intellect of the individual was recognized and encouraged. It was the century when countries like Italy, Spain, and England sent out expeditions to navigate and explore the world, map it, document it, and bring home treasures for the home and the body from exotic places, including porcelains from China, cinnamon from the Spice Islands, silk and cotton kimonos from Japan, and chocolate from Mexico.

These exotic treasures required a place for storage. The edibles went to the kitchen. Silks, ceramics, and lacquerware were placed in a sixteenth century invention, the cabinet, which became an essential piece of furniture. The word cabinet, in architectural language, means "a small room for storing and displaying valuable objects."

And, here's an amusing thought: Did sixteenth century roués say to would-be conquests,"Oh, would you like to come to my cabinet and see my collections?"

of the items inside. In the seventeenth century, they were also made as diplomatic gifts and were often decorated with smooth ivory, semiprecious stones, and perhaps gilt-metal mounts. They often featured impressive marquetry, parquetry, and veneer. They could be painted with Biblical scenes, or the exterior surface was sometimes left simple with the grain of the wood or the intricacy of the inlay becoming the focal point.

Cabinets featured blind doors then. You had to open the door, then the drawer, and pluck the object you wanted to see, or to show to someone. There was something very intriguing about this ritual opening of doors and drawers—a cabinet held secrets, and was all about concealment and revelation. In effect, they were about the power of the person who owned one.

In the eighteenth century, however, the European craze for Chinoiserie led cabinetmakers to insert small glass panels in doors. This way, precious things could be looked at, admired and opinions passed upon their beauty. In Japan, however, the tradition is to keep many of one's

In the sixteenth century, what separated a cabinet from a cupboard was that a cabinet had small, neat drawers and/or pigeon holes to contain precious objects, and a cupboard had shelves. What distinguished it from a chest of drawers is that it had doors.

Early cabinets of the sixteenth century were small, portable, and stood on chests or stands. They measured from five to six feet high, and about three to four feet wide and were designed to be as fancy, ornamental, and exotic as the fancy treasures it contained. Many cabinets were made to store important documents, gold and silver coins of the realm, and other valuable pieces, and their exterior decoration reflected the importance

RIGHT *Logic and simplicity are the rules of design in this kitchen. The glass-front cabinets hold bottles, and the counter below displays the gleaming martini shaker and pitcher used for serving drinks to guests.*

objects concealed, and bring out only a few at a time. This adds to the mystery even more.

Side cabinets are known as credenzas (the Italian word for cabinet) and were designed for the dining room. Many were fitted with glazed doors so that china and other decorative objects could be displayed. These appeared later in the eighteenth century and were made in pairs. Those with shelves above the cabinets were known as chiffoniers.

Curio cabinets keep safe those treasured objects you've been collecting since childhood and cannot bear to throw away. Think of the cabinet as a three-dimensional message board and make it an ever-changing record of your life. Keep curios from travels abroad, things given you by family members, entry tickets from a first-time trip up the Eiffel Tower, and pieces you've acquired on the way, such as small gift cards printed with words you don't want to forget.

If your cabinet shelves have lots of space between them and there is no provision to add more, as is the case in most of the old French pine armoires and Victorian dressers, then build (or get someone to build for you) a set of small stepped

shelves with several levels to keep collections from becoming messy.

Take precise measurements of the space to be filled, making note of the existing shelf's height and depth. Then figure out how many levels will fit into the space between one shelf and the one above it. Draw a pencil sketch on graph paper to figure out the size of the riser. Before you make the final unit you could make a model in light plywood. This will reveal errors in mathematics and avoid costly mistakes.

For the final step unit use lightweight timber and paint (or stain) it the same color as the interior of the existing cabinet. You could also screw a cup hook or two into the underside of the shelf to give you places to hang treasured curios that might look out of place lying flat.

This type of step unit is best served by smaller curios. A toy train engine or a large mask will look too big on the stepped shelves.

When the stepped shelf unit is fitted, and the treasures are in place, you will see a remarkable difference in the way your collection looks.

OPPOSITE *These cabinets were a 5:30 A.M. find in a Paris flea market. Originally a 1920s showcase for ribbons, buttons, and thread, they now hold a mixed collection of unique pieces of nineteenth century glass. The green glasses are Napoleonic; wine was drunk from one end, schnapps from the clear end by Napoleon's troops. Beidermeier and Bauhaus glasses mingle with nineteenth century examples. On top of one cabinet is a unique Bauhaus crystal platter.*

RIGHT *Like is grouped with like: blue glasses together, clear ones together, and the rose-tinted glasses are accent points. Taller pieces are placed in the rear, the shorter ones in front.*

CABINET LIGHTING

Remember that our eyes are in constant motion and that our eyes are more comfortable when a room is lit with many sources of light rather than just one. Lighting for cabinets is easily achieved unless what's stored, like textiles or fragile works of paper, are harmed by light. Stone, ceramics, porcelain, glass, and metal will benefit from dramatic lighting.

- Ideally, the lighting source, whether it's from the top, sides, or front, should be concealed.

- When concealment isn't possible, there are ways to make the lighting discreet, although visible. A miniature low-voltage light can be recessed in the top of a cabinet shelf, and be used with a small metal shield to conceal the light source.

- To make glass sparkle, buy miniature footlights which sit at the front of shelves and throw light on the glass which absorbs and refracts the light. A shadow of the glass object is then enlarged and visible on the back of the shelf.

- If you light glass from the side and the background is dark, the glass, especially faceted glass like Waterford, will glitter.

- If you cast downlights on a glass sculpture, it may absorb the light and refract it. The effect may be as if the glass was lit from within.

- Place glass on a pedestal topped with glass and have uplights concealed within the pedestal. The glass will glow from the uplights.

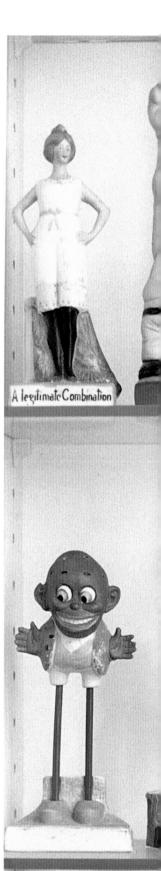

ABOVE *Glass shelves and a white background are a neutral setting for these Schaefer and Vater bisque porcelain figures, circa 1915. They were giveaways. Some were whisky flasks.*

RIGHT *These glass shelves are part of a wall of glass-front cabinets in a bathroom. Each of the witty figures gets its share of the limelight from the subtle interior lighting.*

CABINET STYLES

In the twenty-first century, curio cabinets are not necessarily the luxurious, special pieces of furniture that they were in the sixteenth century. Modern cabinets range from simple, inexpensive grid designs from contemporary design stores to kitchen cupboards found at flea markets and placed not in the kitchen, but in a dining room, hallway or home-office.

A cabinet can be almost anything with doors, transparent or not, with shelves, drawers, or pigeon holes, either singly or in combination. A cabinet is not always a stand-alone piece of furniture. It can be part of an office system, or a 1940s George Nelson mid-century modern sideboard, originally designed as a bar. It can be a country-style pie safe, with a wood-framed punched tin door, or a bird cage constructed of bamboo.

The traditional definition of cabinet is no longer applicable to the twenty-first century edition. The doors to a cabinet can range from opaque to transparent, and can be made of any number of materials, from clear or tinted glass to plastic to wood or perforated stainless steel to wire.

ABOVE *Mickey Mouse in many guises peers out from the glass cabinet, free from dust. His red, black, and white colors are echoed in the art on the wall. The lamp on the floor throws light both on the art and, glancingly, on the mice in the cabinet.*

By placing tiny objects in an equally tiny cabinet, you have organized them, called attention to them, and protected them from getting lost.

A sleek modern cabinet might be made of stainless steel with glass sides and fronts. Or a cabinet can be a tiny display case, a small home for very small objects like miniature chairs, pill or snuff boxes, or cigarette holders.

A Victorian rolltop desk with cubbies and pigeon holes can be transformed into a display cabinet. The drawers can hold flat collectibles, such as botanical specimens mounted on paper, fashion illustrations from the 1950s, or stamps, such as sheets of special issue stamps, still in the original packaging.

ORDINARY & EXTRAORDINARY

A cabinet can be an informal piece of furniture and hold nothing more exceptional than your glasses, dinner plates, and salad bowls. The serious collector, however, usually displays his dinnerware as neatly and graphically as he or she would his or her most precious objects. For the collector, display counts, even when applied to the most ordinary objects such as your local store's wine goblets.

Like all collectibles, dishes and glassware look best grouped like with like. And suddenly the wonderful bulbous shape of a brandy snifter looks particularly voluptuous, while the slender lines of a champagne flute suggest lessons of function dictating form. Striped glasses, designed for orange juice in the 1950s, look lively when seen behind a glass door. Grandma's flower-sprigged porcelain tea cups, maybe once dismissed as fuddy-duddy, also look quaint, delicate, and appealing when placed behind glass.

A true curio cabinet, however, holds surprises. The exterior can be an inexpensive flea market find, a cupboard with glass doors and drawers that you refurbish with a coat of white paint inside and out. But inside, there can be exotica like gleaming mercury balls set gently into

ABOVE *The cabinet filled with Mickey Mouse collectibles can be seen from the sofa, which sits amid a collection of art books that fills three walls of this downstairs den.*

drawers, tortoise shell buttons laid in small drawers, or commemorative silver spoons in honor of an English royal, set out for all to see in a tray.

Cabinets are also good storage places for textiles like antique kimonos and saris. These textiles can be stored flat, wrapped in acid-free paper, and lie horizontally stacked one upon the other for years in a cabinet. Fragile laces, whether on blouses, tablecloths, or linen pillowcases edged in handmade lace, can also be tucked away in a cabinet, to be brought out occasionally to be shown to other textile aficionados. So, too, can rare quilts, Hudson Bay blankets, and embroidered Indian coverlets glittering with mirrors. A glimpse of these colorful

ABOVE *This bed with its extraordinary headboard as cabinet was found in Brittany. Quilts are displayed on it as if it were a settee. Painted Mexican pottery birds are on the shelves. The entire piece of furniture becomes an architectural display case.*

and historic fabrics through a square of glass is tantalizing to a collector.

Many medium-size cabinets, particularly those with opaque doors, are perfect places for irresistible kitsch. Examples might include ephemera like fortunes from Chinese fortune cookies, playbills from twenty years of theater-going, and *The Simpsons* paraphernalia—the dolls of the characters in the television series, brightly designed lunch boxes, and comic books all featuring characters from The Simpsons are worth storing for a future generation. The same can be said of Batman and Superman comics, and *Star Wars* paraphernalia in the 1970s.

ORGANIZING DISPLAYS

Since cabinets come in all different sizes with drawers flat and wide, tall and thin, and because the contents might be as tiny as buttons or cufflinks, the organization can be far more fluid than displays on walls, shelves, and mantels.

If the doors are transparent, the glass panes frame the view, so be very selective about what goes in. If the doors are opaque, you would still use the same design principles as you would on shelves, tablescapes, or mantels. Find a focal point in the center. Even if the shelf opens to reveal a collection of antique men's watches, choose the piece that is the largest and put that in the center

and flank it with the other watches. You will discover another visual attraction because the watch faces will also become focal points.

If the collections on the same shelf are disparate, for example, transparent drinking glasses, different colored glass vases, and silver organize like with like. Group the transparent objects together, the colored ones together, and the silver. Then see how they look next to each other and rearrange accordingly.

When the collectibles are startlingly small, like early twentieth century cufflinks, ivory dice, baby bracelets of silver, jade, and gold, they can fit neatly into drawers, where they can overlap, lie in a pleasant jumble, or if you're super-organized, be divided among tiny partitions lined in velvet.

Occasionally a cabinet will suggest to you which collection would look best. If the cabinet is a printer's tray, then clearly small, flat things like presidential campaign buttons, high school pins, or nineteenth century ladies' hat pins, will fit best. When a cabinet was originally designed to hold papers and layouts for art, it can find a second life as a place to hold a collection of maps, 1940s silk neckties, or sprays of coral. For instance, an apothecary's cabinet, with its many drawers, could hold a collection of feathers, garnet necklaces, or silk ribbons all rolled up in loops.

ABOVE *Delight can be found in the most common objects. Here, three whimsical wood birds are flanked with two children's stackable wood toys in gleaming colors. In the glass-front cabinet like is grouped with like; pairs on the top, trios on the shelf below. On the cupboard shelf are five Fiestaware sugar bowls.*

OPPOSITE *A dental cabinet has the most natural contents, but who would have thought of it? Drills! Dentures! A childhood orthodontic retainer! Scissors fill the drawers, including manicure, first grade, and buttonhole scissors. On top, there are pitchers and teapots with feet all pointing in the same direction as if they were marching off.*

RIGHT *The owner of this apartment is adept at creating visually arresting tableaux, whether on shelves, mantels, or, in this case, a cabinet. He has the tallest object as the focal point, and then the heights diminish, but not predictably.*

THE MORALITY TALE
OF THE CABINET

Once you display something in a cabinet, and think carefully about what goes on behind those closed doors, you begin to think differently about everything else that's behind closed doors from medicine cabinets, to chests of drawers, to the linen closet. As if tidiness was a virus, you may suddenly be caught up in arranging everything, the plaster box, the aspirin bottle, and the toothpaste, in an orderly, graphic fashion. You begin to fold the towels like stores do, with the ends on the inside and only the folded part visible. You roll up your socks, and arrange them side by side, in little balls that are graduated from white to beige to gray to black.

ABOVE *A curved glass display cabinet from a store holds salesman's samples, like hats, shoes, and map tacks, now known as pushpins.*

LEFT *A wonderful collection of objects sits in a Parisian curio cabinet, each item made from papier-mâché.*

BELOW *An antique wood cabinet holds antique glass Christmas ornaments. The balls are contained, while the acorn-shaped ornaments rest on the shelf. The faded quality of both the cabinet and the ornaments is soft and harmonious.*

COLLECTIBLE GLASS

VENETIAN GLASS

The Venetians made glass as early as the tenth century, and in the thirteenth century, the glassmaking factories were moved to Murano. There they make glass goblets, both copies of Renaissance styles and modern ones, that are light in weight, brilliantly colored, and fanciful in shape.

IITTALA GLASSWORKS

Iittala glassworks is a Finnish glasshouse, whose signature designs were made by Aalto, Wirkkala, and Sarpaneva. There is a clean, modern yet organic style to many of the pieces.

DALE CHIHULY

He is one of America's foremost specialists in art glass. His organic sea forms which look like undulating underwater life are particularly famous.

JOSEF HOFFMANN

Josef Hoffmann (1870–1956), the Austrian architect and designer, created furniture, metalwork, and glass. He made exquisite wine and champagne glasses in the 1920s that are fragile and graceful with tulip-shaped bowls on slender, elongated stems. They are so beautiful as to inspire covetousness.

CHRISTMAS ORNAMENTS

The first glass Christmas tree ornaments were made in Germany in the 1860s. They are tiny glass objects of fantasy made in shapes of cows leaping over the moon, angels, pineapples, birds, harlequins, and dogs. They twinkle and they bubble, letting you see some of the joys of Christmas all year.

COLLECTIBLE POTTERY

Pottery is fragile and for practical reasons it should be tucked into a cabinet. But if you are a blithe spirit, it can also be used at meals. Here are a few collectibles that would look good in your cabinet.

CLARICE CLIFF

Anything by pottery designer Clarice Cliff, (1899–1972) who worked in several English factories after the 1920s, including Royal Staffordshire Pottery, and designed brilliantly colored Art Deco patterns. Most famous were the hand-painted "Bizarre" series.

PABLO PICASSO

Anything by artist Pablo Picasso (1881–1973). In 1947, Picasso worked in the Madoura pottery of Suzanne and Georges Ramie in Vallauris, France, and made original statues, human heads, and vessels. He also painted plates and jugs.

LUSTERWARE

Lusterware is pottery with an iridescent metallic surface first developed by Egyptian glass painters in the seventh and eighth centuries. It was then applied to pottery in places like Baghdad by the ninth and tenth centuries. The pigments were made from metallic oxides such as copper to produce ruby red, that was then applied to the glazed surface, and then re-fired. It is still made today.

RUSSEL WRIGHT

Russel Wright (1904–1976), an American industrial designer, made biomorphic-shaped tableware at the Steubenville Pottery, and porcelain kitchen-ware with indentations rather than handles. His color palette included gray, pink, and chartreuse.

ABOVE *Placed at an angle, this Memphis-style cabinet presents a Warhol vase on its top shelf, and more works by the artist hang on the walls.*

RIGHT *This angular cabinet in an entrance hall displays works by Ettore Sottsass, Matteo Thun, and Masanori Umeda of the Memphis design group. The startling red piece is by Sottsass. A pleasing symmetry prevails with an overhead light shining top center to grab the eye. On the floor, guarding the pieces, plaster dogs sit, alert.*

Light Wells

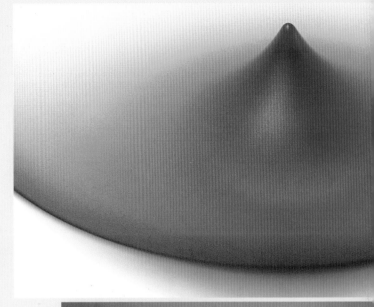

Once a collection is arranged, it has to be lit for the eye to automatically focus on the objects. A collection sequestered in darkness might as well be invisible.

Light comes in many types: as warm incandescent, colder but sparkly halogen, cold fluorescent, and fiber optics. The latter has a single light source placed in a box. A reflector focuses the light down single glass fibers, which give off light at the end.

Decide if you want uplights, downlights, pin lights, or light on tracks. Fittings can be situated on the floor as an uplight, or in the ceiling to focus down. Single bulbs can be recessed into walls, floors, shelves, and cabinets, and also in tiny strips, which can be glued or nailed to the display system. Small light fittings can be inserted at the top, bottom, or sides of shelves, walls, and display cabinets.

Where you place light is determined by what you want to emphasize. For example, if the collection is laid out in a grid, light the objects so light falls on the front of the objects.

Fiber optics can be wired to go in dozens of directions. Track lighting has flexibility. The least flexible is a framing projector, which is usually concealed in a ceiling. A lighting technician cuts a copper mask with a tiny opening so the light falls exactly on the object.

Stone, metals, and ceramics can take bright lighting. Textiles and works on paper will fade in the presence of bright light. For antique embroideries, photography, and lithographs, use low voltage lights.

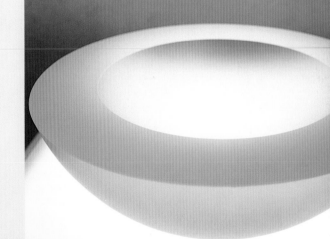

OPPOSITE *Here, gentle lighting falls on the front of the works of art to highlight but not damage them. The female form is placed in front of the painting, so it becomes a small study of the female nude. Decoys on the wall are lit from the ceiling.*

LEFT *The man on the shelf is lit directly by a spot from track lighting on the ceiling. The room is lit with a lot of general lighting, too, and the spot brings the antique wood sculpture more into focus.*

RIGHT *A combination of uplighters and spotlights from ceiling mounted track lighting brings each work of art and piece of sculpture into its own in this loft space. Each light switch is fitted with a dimmer so that the amount of light can be changed as desired.*

OPPOSITE *This display of blue and white ceramics is lit from the top. The light goes through the glass shelves, illuminating the entire cabinet. The objects are arranged in a symmetry with lots of space between them so the light is not blocked.*

RIGHT *The architect inserted a row of tiny low-voltage lights under the shelves holding this display. The lights do two things. They light what lies below, and they make the shelf appear to float.*

OPPOSITE *A huge piece of art glass by Stanislav Libensky and Jaroslava Brychtova has its own plinth, which in turn is on a platform, designed to catch the natural light pouring in the window. The apartment faces Manhattan's Central Park, and the light from morning to dusk dazzles.*

ABOVE *Natural light shines through the blue glass bottles on shelves set in a window. The shapes of the bottles stand out against the clear glass and in their verticality, appear to echo the cityscape outside.*

Whether you love to collect
china frogs or Mao buttons
or colored eggs, these collections
intrigue and delight the eye.

Magnificent
Obsessions

Colorful Mexican rebozos cover the backs of chairs for a special dining occasion.

Some people are so enamored of collecting that it becomes a wonderful, addictive, lifetime obsession, and the home becomes a three-dimensional, highly tactile reflection of that obsession. When you enter the room of an avid collector you know you have encountered a person of passion, of confidence, and of unbridled enthusiasms. You have not just entered a home, you are privy to a joyous mania.

Those who are obsessed display their collections often from floor to ceiling, wall to wall, and room to room. However, they do not do clutter! They display their collections with an extravagant but careful eye, and know the provenance, the fables, and all the facts about each of their possessions. These mild obsessives have been known to take telephone calls at 3:00 A.M. concerning a special find in a flea market. They will then get out of bed in their night attire, throw on a coat and travel to see

this holy grail in person. Yes, you could say they were eccentric but nice.
For this chapter, and indeed for the entire book, some very special people
were interviewed, collectors who love to collect. Like most people, they
were refreshingly honest about their passions, about the small and large
objects of their affection.

How they displayed these objects, decorated their entire home with
them was, as you will see, highly individual. Beginning with a collection
of brightly colored fringed scarves and a collection of Mexicana that
reminds the owner of exactly where she comes from, bringing with it all
the joys of family, the chapter moves on to look at the passion of a
Parisian interior designer whose name is synonymous with Belle Epoque
style. American quilts follow this flight of fantasy, and they in turn are
followed by the multiple collections of a professional curator.

OPPOSITE LEFT *The beaded African chair was at an antiques center in Manhattan and Ms. Martinez bought it immediately.*

OPPOSITE RIGHT

On this Mexican wire tree, she has suspended part of her collection of hearts including a heart-shaped tea strainer, a ceramic one with an arrow, and one of mirrored tin.

ABOVE *This small room is clearly the warmest room in the house. An embroidered textile is above the fireplace, an oversized acrylic shoe is decorated with oranges, lemons, grapefruit, and plums.*

Zarela Martinez has been collecting things Mexican since she was in her twenties. As a cookery author and owner of a restaurant, she is a force of nature, imaginative, and generous. Her home is filled with brilliant colors and textures, and exceptional comfort.

Zarela firmly believes there is no point in having something if you aren't going to use it on a daily basis. Take *rebozos*, Mexican rectangular wraps made of rayon or silk which have many uses. They can be worn as scarves, shawls, or skirts. Women carry their babies in them and Zarela, who has forty of them, has wrapped them around casseroles. Men weave the body of the *rebozos*, and women the fringe. Those made of silk have to be able to pass through a wedding ring.

She also has a passion for *serapes*, which she tosses over sofas, layering one over the other, creating cheerful color and comfort zones.

Zarela is also enamored of beaded Mexican pillows called *huichol*, and owns a stunning beaded African chair. She also collects outfits from Chiapas, intricately embroidered with figures of roses and deer. (In Chiapas, a woman cannot get married until she can weave an outfit for herself and one for her husband.)

Here's a Latin American passion seen amid a reverie of red.

Like most people in the throes of a magnificent obsession, Parisian interior designer Pierre Pothier, the designer of the Belle Epoque interior of Maxim's de Paris, and of the interior of a cruise ship belonging to part of the Maxim group, is a firm believer in over-the-top design. Nothing is too much in terms of pattern and texture.

He understands the art of flamboyance and extravagance and practices it without inhibition for hotels, private clients, and naturally, as you can see here, at home.

When his extraordinary work was included in the "La Belle Epoque" exhibition at the Metropolitan Museum of Art in Manhattan, he received a letter from the famous style arbiter, Diana Vreeland, which read, "You are a magician." She is absolutely right.

Pierre Pothier abhors a blank wall, particularly in restaurants, where he believes that a diner's eye shouldn't be still for a moment. If a customer sees a bare wall, there is the possibility he will start thinking about his taxes or about how his son smashed up the car. These thoughts are not welcome during lunch or dinner.

His private passions are far-ranging. When he was younger (he is now in that time of his life when he can be called ageless), he lived for three years in Tahiti and like the French painter before him, Gauguin, Pierre became enamored of Polynesian sculptures and seashells in their infinite varieties, from those the size of fingernails to those of the backs of tortoises.

This penthouse apartment is a fine example of how to decorate your living space with the things you love. He has not given up one iota of his passion for color, texture, and for Polynesia. He has been uncompromising. Even stuffed animal heads on the wall dividing the living room from the kitchen are framed with spiky deep sea shells. The deep turquoise color of the lacquered dining table

ABOVE *At Pierre Pothier's richly textured apartment, dozens upon dozens of shells from Tahiti and Bora Bora sit on the glass shelves, while a giant turtle shell demands instant attention.*

OPPOSITE *Looking across the dining table, he practices in his home what he preaches about restaurant design. The eye should never be still. A pair of faux buffalo horns are on a side table. Above the hatch are copies of guns made for Louis XV.*

reflects that of the ocean. This exotic table is a collector's item and is designed especially for this small space. When guests arrive, chairs are taken out from the table and slotted back in when the dinner is over. It's all in the design.

The lounge seating area covers one-half of this room. A raised area is covered with extra large cushion pads that are covered with highly patterned throws. On top of the fabric throws, pillows of different shapes and sizes are casually placed, inviting the guest to sit, sprawl, or lie in comfort, as if back in a Pacific paradise.

Lighting is low, almost nonexistent. Lamps place low focus on different areas of the collection to suit the desired mood. Otherwise, the mood is calm and mysterious, ideal for relaxing and taking in the unique ambience.

It is not just that Ana Daniel has twenty quilts, mostly American, that makes her collection extraordinary. It is how she uses each of them to decorate her 1860s farmhouse and barn on Long Island that is so alluring.

She displays them so that they are almost on an equal par with the architecture. In her hands, these fragile, antique textiles have a graphic presence integral to the house.

Her passion for quilts came from a liking for Americana. She related to the habit that woman of the pioneering age had of keeping rag bags. Those rags were the pieces that became quilts. Nothing went to waste. Like those who made the quilts, Ms. Daniel does not buy anything she cannot use. For her, the quilts and her home, a New England, shingle-style 1860s farmhouse, are

a perfect match of like with like. Quilts are used as covers on beds in each of the guest rooms, which adds to the country feel of her home. The colors in each of the quilts are a complement to the golden timber surfaces: the wide-planked walls, the cross beams, and the high ceiling are all of country timber that has an aged patina, like the quilts.

HANGING UP

To successfully hang these quilts on the wall, a binding was attached to the back of the quilt at the top, and a rod was carefully fed through it so the quilt could hang without being stretched out of shape. This is a simple process that can be carried out either by a quiltmaker, or you could try to do it yourself, if you have the right tools and equipment.

You would need a strong binding of the correct width, strong thread with which to sew it on a sewing machine, and a wooden rod slightly less wide than the width of the binding so it can slip through the stitched binding easily. Measure both the rod and the binding accurately. Then measure the width of the quilt and cut both the strip of binding and the light piece of wood to length. Your local lumber or craft store will advise you as to which type to buy. To hang it, tie the selected rope onto both ends of the rod and put in place.

PLACING IT

If the quilt is large and colorful, hang it on a large wall in a spacious room, or it will loom too large in the scheme of things. Do not hang it in a place where people walk past. They will brush against it, and it will get damaged. Also, be wary of sunlight because this will also cause damage. A magnificent obsession does not have to be

about truly magnificent things, like scholars' rocks, Gobelins tapestries, or Van Gogh paintings. Hélène Verin, a designer of wall coverings, textiles and furniture, collects serious things like art by Joseph Beuys, textiles by Jack Lenor Larsen, and some very unserious things like Hermès boxes. She is happy to receive one of their boxes with a present tucked inside. She is equally happy to get them empty. It is the color and the packaging that delight her visual sense.

To her, orange is the greatest color in the world She's not a primary color kind of gal. Orange is warm, sunny, and vibrant. Sometimes she piles her boxes up in a stack in her loft as a dominating still life or, as she described it one winter's day, "a Hanukkah bush for a Jewish princess."

Her example of how you can make a mountain out of boxes proves you can display anything.

ABOVE LEFT *This vibrant cache of boxes, ranging from giant prop boxes to flat ones for scarves, is stacked up as an orange still life. Its color certainly adds personality to this area of the loft.*

ABOVE RIGHT *The vest is decorated with some of the hundreds of fashion labels the owner has saved over the decades.*

Barbara Schubeck, an art director, collects hundreds of labels for clothes. Carol Horn, Cacharel, Original by Wilkinson, Sy Devore of Hollywood, Irish Tweed, A. Smile Inc., Grin & Wear It are just a sample of the names.

This is a woman who has picked labels off the sidewalk. As an art director, she is intrigued by the graphic design. The designers of labels must make the type interesting, readable, and memorable in such a small space (measuring one and a half inches by three-quarter of an inch). For several years, she hoarded the labels, drew up a layout for the labels, and planned to put them on a vest.

Finally, her patient husband purchased a plain beige-colored vest for her, then took charge of the layouts. He found a dressmaker to sew the labels on the vest according to her design. The result is this wearable collectible.

Does she wear it? You bet.

She is a person who is interested in things that other people are not. That is how Dorothy Twining Globus, a former director of the Museum at the Fashion Institute of Technology in Manhattan, and the Curator of Exhibitions at the Cooper-Hewitt National Design Museum, talks about her passion for collectibles.

She has curated museum shows on shopping bags, playing cards, and annual reports and a retrospective of the work of costume and fashion designer, Bob Mackie, who designed for stars such as Cher and Carol Burnett.

She has also been described as a collector of the unloved thing, which she collects and regroups as families thus making them into loved ones. By grouping any of these objects with its kith and kin, she finds the narrative, the thread, and the permutations of design of any single object.

What she sees is people's desire to invent things practical and impractical, to improve and diversify. Dorothy sees design in the smallest object and is interested in the continuum.

Those unloved, ignored things which fill her apartment are all arranged in brilliant groupings of like with like, but are interjected with visual wit and puns. They include staplers and erasers, insulators, and baby formula bottles. She has buttons loose and on their original cards, paper clips and thumbtacks, pens and pencils.

There are foldable hangers for travel, children's hangers in pastel pink, blue, and yellow, and dolly hangers. She has telegrams. "There's something compelling about the yellow telegram," she said. "It's usually bad news, but it was exciting if it was a birthday telegram, a thanksgiving telegram, or a mother's day telegram."

As a curator, she codifies and sorts her objects, and, especially, understands the reasons for their design. Take a carpenter pencil. "It was flat, so as not to roll on the job."

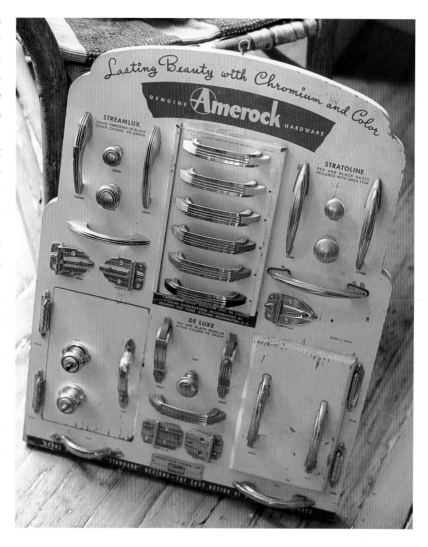

ABOVE *In handles lies diversity. This is a fine example of a 1950s salesman's sample of handles for kitchen cupboards. Chromium was all the rage then and the science of ergonomics was in its infancy.*

Her home is astonishingly full of extraordinary visual tableaux. In placing the collections she looks for balance and comfort. Interestingly, she uses odd numbers, believing asymmetry to be more natural. And she thinks about the placement. In her apartment, which she shares with both her husband and their daughter, everywhere there is a story. Focal point in one area of living space, on top of a cabinet of drawers, is a great collection of buildings. Downtown Manhattan with a few exotica thrown in, such as the Taj Mahal and Notre Dame, amuses guests and friends. The cast of characters in this tableau includes metal boats, with piers and docks from a 1950s children's toy made by Tri-ang, an English company. Although there are more Woolworth and Empire State buildings than Citicorp buildings, for instance, there is a logic to this scene. From left to right, it is going south to north.

The collector in her sees value in things as small as buttons, collar stays, and shoe and belt buckles. What she perceives is social history. Dorothy understands that if you gather together enough varieties of the simplest thing, you will discover material culture, innovation, and the occasional product with a touch of goofiness.

Take beads. When she organizes a collection, she places like with like, and within that, subdivides into even smaller categories, sometimes by color. In a type case, used in the days when books and papers were printed with hot type, she has filled one drawer's tiny divisions with beads organized by color—clear, coral, yellow, green. Within the colors, she has sorted them by birds, domestic animals, and wild animals.

ABOVE *A collector organizes disparate objects by grouping like with like, by seeing what fits into the shallow recesses. Dice large and small are together, with balls underneath.*

LEFT *Globes big and small, and all out-of-date, are organized with the largest in the back, and in descending order of size. The globes are useless for using to study geography now, but they tell a story of conquest and defeat.*

OPPOSITE *A scene from the waterfront in New York's harbor. In the drawers below buttons are sorted by color.*

This collection of minutiae reveals the joy of colors, a variety of materials (plastic, Bakelite, ceramic, mother-of-pearl) and an almost infinite number of designs.

If possible, she tries to collect minutiae in their original state, like buttons still sewn onto cards, straight pins on cards, hooks and eyes on cards. The cards are examples of graphic design, whether they're Woolworth's cards with a mosaic design, or another card that looks like Doric columns. By the design and colors, she will know the era.

In the 1950s, for example, two voguish colors were avocado and a burnt orange. So when those colors pop up on jewelry, radios, dresses, or kitchen handles, you can guess the era with some certainty. If buttons in those colors come attached to cards with biomorphic patterns, that extra bit of information dates the buttons to the 1950s more firmly and reassures a collector.

The more information you get, the more satisfying collecting becomes, because a decade of design becomes clearer.

How to
Start a
Collection

It's astonishing how a significant collection can begin with just one item such as a book, a vase, or a photograph.

Glass

- Tiffany glass lamp shades are still highly sought-after pieces.

- Venetian Art Glass is usually stamped for verification. Look for a stamp under the piece.

- Consider collecting retro (1950s and 1960s) Scandinavian and Italian glass vases and bowls for their color, form, and texture. Look for names such as Flygsfors, Orrefors, and Sarpaneva.

LEFT *Color and form make this grouping visually appealing. It sits on a window ledge so the natural light plays with the color reflections, creating different effects during the day and early evening.*

Glass is so alluring. It comes in astonishing colors, from clear to claret to cobalt; it can be hand-blown or molded, and can have swirls, stripes, and dots. Items made from glass can be functional, such as a flower vase, a drinking goblet, or a pitcher. Or it can be solely decorative, such as an art piece created by glass artist Dale Chihuly.

A collection can start simply. A flea market find of a set of cobalt Russian tea glasses, intricately decorated with a gold filigree; or you are in Venice and take a boat to Murano, where you get to see glassblowers practice a delicate craft that dates to the thirteenth century.

There are many different types of glass to collect, including cute Early American Pattern Glass (made from the mid-1820s to around 1915), Victorian glassware, vintage milk glass, colored medicine bottles, and Depression Era glassware. Elegant European glass vases and accessories from manufacturers such as Lalique, Baccarat, and Daum are also worthwhile collectibles.

Items to collect include colorful patterned paperweights, perfume and scent bottles, and small glass figures of people, animals, and plants. There are specific interest areas, too, such as horse racing. Derby glass celebrates this sport of kings.

Exhibitions of art glass are held in galleries all the time. Ask advice from an art glass dealer as to what is collectible in your corner of the world.

Lastly, learn why something is valuable. Ask questions and always get a bill of sale.

Americana

- If animated cartoons by Walt Disney or Chuck Jones are too expensive, consider younger animators such as Matt Groening who created *The Simpsons*.

- Check that folk art such as decoys, quilts, and samplers are genuine.

- Some people collect the newly obsolete which includes ashtrays, computers, and both manual and early electric typewriters.

RIGHT *This Native American piece sits on a specially constructed plinth jutting out from a white wall in the foyer of a modern home. The piece is a Hopi butterfly maiden kachina dated circa 1920.*

Americana can encompass anything from *"I Like Ike"* buttons to duck decoys to quilts selling for hundreds of thousands of dollars. It also includes outsider art or self-taught art, which is usually reasonably priced.

Early Navajo blankets, Hudson Bay blankets, and Pendleton blankets are other examples of Americana. Some of these collectibles are already expensive, such as old Amish quilts, which can sell for thousands of dollars.

An alternative might be to buy new Amish quilts or patchwork quilts from the 1920s, which sell for hundreds, not thousands, of dollars. Also, perhaps collect new quilts by an upcoming artisan you see at a crafts fair. Always consult a dealer if you intend to buy as an investment.

Toys

Any of these names bring back memories? Lionel trains, Mickey Mouse, Barbie dolls, Tri-ang, and Matchbox cars. The toys of our youth can hold a nostalgic allure for us as adults.

Tin toys, battery-operated toys, and friction toys are all collectible. A new plastic friction Ferrari car may sell for twelve dollars, but a pressed steel Lincoln sedan recently sold for more than $6,000. Bisque, china, rubber and plastic dolls, and teddy bears, of course, are also sought-after.

Items such as Matchbox cars, Smurfs, Beanies, Star Wars, Star Trek, Walt Disney characters, and The Simpsons memorabilia are traded regularly. Buy antique toys for yourself. Young children do not appreciate a $200 wind-up toy that they can't play with everyday.

ABOVE LEFT *Mickey Mouse is a perennial favorite collectible. Keep precious rag Mickey Mouses in a display cabinet, away from dust and pollution.*

ABOVE RIGHT *A 1940s wood and aluminum wind tunnel model of a jet is jauntily suspended from a skylight in a stairwell leading to an upper bedroom.*

- Toys in their original packaging are worth more than those that are not.

- Barbie dolls have clothes, furniture, and more as added collectibles.

- Bears to collect include those from North American Bear Company, Gund, Paddington, Steiff, and Muffy.

- Fisher-Price toys were made of wood from 1931 to 1950, but by 1964 they were almost completely plastic.

Silver

- Look for the silver mark on a piece of antique silver to verfiy its maker.

- If washed and dried by hand and kept in a tarnish-proof box, silver will maintain its sheen for decades.

- Missing pieces from a set of sterling silver flatware? Try one of the many silver-matching services to replace it before you despair.

Silver is a lovely metal that does not lose its attraction as it ages. The desire to begin to collect silver, whether for jewelry, flatware, or as decorative pieces, can start unostentatiously.

The desire to own sterling silver flatware may start upon the inheritance of your grandmother's set. Suddenly, it seems that the service needs a few more pieces, another gravy ladle, an extra serving spoon. You can become greedy in the nicest way.

Any item made of sterling silver has the words "Sterling Silver" on the back of it, along with the name of the manufacturer or a mark denoting a certain era. You cannot be defrauded buying silver because the maker's mark is indelible.

Look for pieces either made in a specific period, for example, Art Deco, or by the same designer or manufacturer. These will generally improve their value more than work by any of the lesser-known silversmiths, especially if in good condition.

Perhaps start with 1920s and 1930s smoking paraphernalia such as cigarette cases and lighters. Candleholders, extravagant candelabras, silver boxes, visiting card holders, letter openers, bar accessories such as original cocktail shakers and corkscrews, hip flasks, and salt and pepper shakers are objects you can pick up at local antiques fairs and markets for reasonable prices.

If you decide to collect silver jewelry made in the 1900s, consider collecting only pieces by the same jewelry designer. By doing this you can create a cohesive collection and reflects his or her life's work. As such, it can be worth more in the future.

Photographs

- Start a photography collection by buying postcards, stereo cards, or daguerreotypes.

- A small Eliot Porter photograph of a bird recently sold for $2,390; a Margaret Bourke-White image of the Hudson River Bridge sold for $8,365 and a Man Ray sold for $339,950.

- Display framed photographs in places away from direct sunlight.

ABOVE *This series of drawings by Robert Longo on vellum have been chosen for the similarity in style and have each been framed in the same black framing material. They are a highly personal collection and enliven a large wall space with personality.*

Photographs are not only less expensive than paintings and sculpture, they are usually more understandable, particularly if you like portraits, landscapes, or street scenes. George Platt Lyne, Edward Weston and Diane Arbus are names that conjure up specific styles of photography.

You can begin a collection of photography by haunting flea markets and buying Victorian albums. Stereo cards, post cards of exotica like the world's Chinatowns, landmarks of the world like the Eiffel Tower, or images of delicious fruit, like giant grapefruits, oranges, and watermelons are also good collectibles. Your collection might begin with a trove of family heirloom photographs, handed down through generations. These images reveal a social as well as personal history.

With photography, it is a matter of what type of images you like. Photographs by the early greats, for example, Steichen, Berenice Abbott, and Brassaï are collectible. Or leap into buying today's photographers, and buy names such as Sebastião Salgado and David LaChapelle. Some of the works by Magnum photographers are worth collecting, as is anything by fashion photographers such as Herb Ritts, Steven Meisel, and Bruce Weber. Prices of photographs range from under $100 to hundreds of thousands of dollars.

The Library of Congress sells photographs taken by Walker Evans as part of the (then) Federal Works Progress Administration in the 1930s—an eight-by-ten inch print costs about $18, an eleven-by-fourteen inch costs about $25.

RIGHT *This is the room of a true bibliophile, and it is a booklover's dream to have so many shelves! The books are displayed in an orderly manner and the ladder gives easy access to those placed on the high shelves. The books have been placed away from damaging direct sunlight.*

Books

- First editions with the original cover and in mint condition are the most valuable.

- Signed copies are preferable and more valuable than unsigned copies.

- Collect secondhand books either by topic, for example, early illustrated works on flora and fauna, or books by the same author to create a worthwhile investment.

A book collection should be a natural thing, something not created by your interior designer who orders you Plato, Aristotle, and all of Shakespeare, bound in leather, which you or your family will never read.

A book collection starts with your first book, even if was a children's book. Battered paperbacks can perhaps be given away, but hardcovers, and a series of paperbacks from the same publisher or author, for example, all of Patricia Highsmith, William Faulkner, and Gabriel Garcia Marquez can be grouped together.

Look for first editions of your favorite books, for example, Ernest Hemingway's *The Old Man and the Sea*, F. Scott Fitzgerald's *The Great Gatsby*, and Gabriel García Márquez's *One Hundred Years of Solitude* and plan your collection around these authors. Nowadays a signed first edition of any book by J. R. R. Tolkien would be a coup. Recently, the *Lord of the Rings* trilogy, inscribed to Michael H. R. Tolkien, the author's son, sold for $152,500.

In 2002 a Manhattan auction house sold a private library for about seven million dollars. Many of the books were inscribed by the authors to friends and family, including a copy of *Lolita* inscribed by Vladimir Nabokov to his wife Véra.

Ezra Pound inscribed a copy of *A Draft of XVI Cantos of Ezra Pound for the Beginning of a Poem of Some Length* to Olga Rudge, a violin player, who was Pound's companion for many years. The inscripton reads: "Dear Olga. This is your copy. Ezra."

Acknowledgments

For their expertise and friendship, I want to thank David McFadden, senior curator, Museum of Arts and Design in New York City; Kate Carmel, formerly acting director of the American Crafts Museum (now Museum of Arts and Design); Ralph and Terry Kovel; William Lipton and Yvonne Wong; Lark Mason, senior vice president, Sotheby's, New York City; Matthew Weigman, also of Sotheby's; Deborah Sussman and Paul Prejza; Tom Woodard and Blanche Greenstein; David Weingarten; and Lucia Howard.

Thanks to Michael Cannell, my editor at the *New York Times*, for allowing me to do this book, Claude Lapeyre for taking wonderful pictures, Mary Staples for designing an airy book that tells a clear story, and to Sterling Publishing for liking the idea, and Lynn Bryan for her expertise and contagious enthusiasm.

And, thanks to Anna Sussman and Robert Grossman for their sweet support.

Index